KU-325-927

© Michael T.R.B. Turnbull, 1989

Published by W & R Chambers Ltd Edinburgh, 1989

British Library Cataloguing in Publication Data

Turnbull, Michael, *1941-*
  Edinburgh monuments and statues.—
  (Chambers mini guides).
  1. Edinburgh. Monuments
  I. Title
  941.3'4

  ISBN 0-550-20050-9

Cover design by John Marshall

Typeset by Bookworm Typesetting Ltd, Edinburgh
Printed in Singapore by
Singapore National Printers Ltd

MONUMENTS
AND
STATUES
OF
EDINBURGH

Michael T.R.B. Turnbull

Chambers

Contents

Preface

The statues of Edinburgh, beginning with the oldest, the lead equestrian portrait of Charles II, are (with only a few exceptions) the images of national figures. The 60 statues described in this book are the major public statues of the city. The many statues and busts displayed in institutions to which public access is not easily available have generally not been described.

For the purposes of this book, monuments have been distinguished from portrait statues as being memorials in which actual historical figures are not represented and which feature only generalised images of the human figure. Wells, fountains and stones have also been included as forms of public monument (but descriptions of these are not given). Cross-references are given in cases where more than one statue or monument exists for the same person or persons (the Covenanters, for example, are commemorated both in the Martyrs Cross (Grassmarket) and in the Covenanters Monument).

Monuments and statues are associated not only with churchyard memorials; with its wealth of public statuary and the range and grandeur of its monuments, Edinburgh is of particular interest to the visitor. What is surprising, however, is that there exists no large-scale outdoor public memorial to honour Mary Queen of Scots, in spite of her historical significance and the attraction of her life-story to tourists.

Of all the sculptors who have embellished the city, one, Sir John Steell, stands head and shoulders above the rest for his enormous and consistently impressive output. It is all the more ironical, therefore, that this tireless craftsman, who contributed so much to Edinburgh's visual distinction, should lie in a grave in Old Calton Cemetery that is faceless and bare.

Familiar landmarks, statues and monuments, become unrecognised with time, melting into the accepted texture of our daily lives, only occasionally acknowledged by chance or at infrequent anniversaries. Yet each statue and each monument is the product of personal or collective loss; they exist because it was believed that the persons they commemorate should be remembered by future generations. And *we* are those generations.

Note

The precise location of Edinburgh's monuments and statues is clearly indicated in the text, which is arranged in alphabetical order. The section *Finding your Way About* at the back of the book groups the monuments and statues into convenient area locations. However, readers and visitors to the city would be well advised to use this book in conjunction with a good map. This done, there should be little difficulty in locating the monuments and statues described.

Michael T.R.B. Turnbull

I should like to acknowledge in particular the advice and help given to me by my colleague, the late Alasdair MacCallum, and the support I have received from the staff of the Edinburgh Room of the Central Library, George IV Bridge, Edinburgh.

Select Reading List

General

The Buildings of Scotland: Edinburgh, Eds. John Gifford, Colin McWilliam and David Walker, Penguin, 1984

Edinburgh Portraits, M Turnbull, John Donald Publishers Ltd, 1987

Monuments and Statues

Civic Stone, I R Simpson and C Stephen, Scotland's Cultural Heritage, 1982

An Edinburgh Miscellany, W F Gray, Robert Grant and Son, 1925

To Barbara

Monuments

72nd Duke of Albany's Own Highlanders

Castle Esplanade: top north-west corner

A red granite obelisk erected by the Regiment commemorates men killed in action or who died of wounds or disease during the campaign in Afghanistan in 1878-80. The Peterhead granite monument is the work of McDonald, Field & Co. (1882-83).

The regiment was originally raised as the Earl of Seaforth's Regiment in 1778. In 1823 (having been deprived of the kilt) the regiment was again made a Highland one and in the following year it returned to Scotland and was quartered at Edinburgh Castle after an absence of 24 years. Recruitment for the 72nd began in the Highlands and a unique new uniform was designed: Royal Stuart tartan trews, red coatees and feather bonnets.

On 1 August 1825 new colours were presented to the regiment on Bruntsfield Links, with a new regimental badge: the cipher 'F' and the coronet of Prince Frederick, Duke of York and Albany (whose magnificent statue can be seen only a few feet away (see STATUES).

The Afghan campaign of 1877 was made necessary because the Afghans had accepted a Russian embassy and refused the British Mission in Kabul. The British Government decided that a Mission had to be established and that, if necessary, force would be used.

In November Major-General Frederick Roberts VC led a force into Afghanistan and was faced by a hostile army on Peiwar Kotal Pass. On 2 December the right wing, composed of the 72nd Highlanders and the 5th Gurkhas, stormed the flank by night and captured 21 enemy guns.

A severe winter was followed in May by the Treaty of Gandamach, by which the Afghans accepted the setting up of a British Mission. However, six weeks later the staff of the Mission were massacred. General Roberts was ordered to occupy Kabul.

An Afghan army of 12000 blocked the passage of the British Army in October; again the 72nd and the Gurkhas made a flank attack. At Charasiah the regiment carried its colours into battle for the last time. On 13 October General Roberts entered Kabul (with 200 captured guns and 7000 enemy rifles), marching through the city to the music of military bands.

In December 1879 the 72nd was encamped outside Kabul when a Holy War (Jehad) was declared. The regiment was then active in the hills around the city. On 14 December, during fighting, Lance-Corporal George Sellar had gone ahead armed with rifle and bayonet and in hand-to-hand combat was severely wounded by an Afghan with a knife. General Roberts had watched the incident through his binoculars and Lance-Corporal Sellar was later awarded the VC. A 300-mile march was ordered in 1880; the temperature rose to 110 at midday and fell to freezing at midnight. For 22 days the army marched with no losses among the 10000 troops, 11000 animals and 8000 camp followers. On 1 September they attacked the Afghan army at Kandahar; the 72nd were part of the left flank. In the battle two officers of the regiment (including the Commanding Officer) and eleven men were killed.

Black Watch
The Mound: top of Market Street

An imposing eleven-foot bronze statue of a soldier (by Birnie Rhind) guards the junction of the Mound with Market Street: leaning on a rifle, he looks out across Edinburgh to the River Forth.

When the statue on its red granite pedestal was unveiled early on the morning of 25 May 1910 it had for background a tree just coming into leaf. There was no public ceremony as the nation was in mourning for the death of King Edward VII on 6 May. The sun shone and the memorial was very much admired by many people passing. On the pedestal are plaques with the names of the more than 200 men of the Black Watch who died or were wounded in the South African War; a large bronze relief shows soldiers of the regiment launching an attack. Among those named is General Wauchope who was killed at Magersfontein Hill along with 46 officers and 706 men of the Highland Brigade. In 1900 the regiment suffered many casualties at Paardeburg.

The oldest Highland regiment, the Black Watch was formed in 1739 from the companies of Highlanders raised by General Wade to help contain the Highlands. The 43rd or Highland Regiment of Foot acquired the name of 'Black Watch' from their being permitted to wear the forbidden tartan, its dark green contrasting with the bright colour of the Redcoats.

The exploits of the Black Watch are legendary, from the Battle of Fontenoy in 1745 (where they used the tactic of loading, waiting for the enemy to raise their rifles, then falling flat to the ground before they fired, getting up quickly, firing a volley and attacking with sword and shield) to the campaigns against the French in the Low Countries in 1793, when it was so cold that birds dropped dead from the trees and horses lay lifeless, still harnessed to their ice-bound guns and wagons.

Brassfounders of Leith

Nicolson Square

In the centre of the garden is a pillar surmounted by a small statue of a brassfounder by John S Rhind (1859-1937). The pillar was designed by James Gowans, Lord Dean of Guild, for the International Exhibition of Industry, Science and Art held on the West Meadows of Edinburgh in 1886 (where the monument won a gold medal).

The statue on the top of the pillar is of Tubal Cain mentioned in the Bible (Genesis 4.22) as an 'instructor of every artificer in brass and iron'. The 24 bronze plaques are of heraldic devices, castles, military and church figures, nations of Britain, the Royal Burghs of Scotland and the Brassfounders Guild of Edinburgh and Leith. The statue is 4 ft high and stands on a 16-ft pillar: the complete monument is made up of some 4 hundredweight of bronze.

Burns Monument

Regent Road: south side

Overlooking New Calton Cemetery, the Burns Monument by Thomas Hamilton (1830) is a variation on his earlier monument to the poet at Alloway (1820).

Originally the Edinburgh Burns Monument contained in its base the marble statue of the poet by John Flaxman (1755-1826) which is now to be found in the Scottish National Portrait Gallery. It also contained relics of Burns – these are now in Lady Stair's House.

Burns Monument

Covenanters Monument

Redford Road: outside Dreghorn Barracks

The monument (like the Drummond Scrolls at Redford House on the other side of the road) is constructed from the most highly-worked features of the facade of William Adam's Royal Infirmary.

In this case four Ionic columns have been placed back-to-back to form an imposing if eccentric landmark. Beside the monument is a long and rambling inscription in verse marking the site as having seen Romans, Jacobites and Covenanters march or ride by.

The monument was erected at the instructions of R A Macfie of Dreghorn. (*See also*: Martyrs Cross MONUMENTS).

The Floral Clock

West Princes Street Gardens

The Floral Clock, the invention of John McHattie, Edinburgh Parks Superintendent, first delighted visitors and citizens in the spring of 1904. It was constructed by Messrs James Ritchie & Sons Ltd from the old turret clock of Elie Parish Church, Fife, and this mechanism lasted till 1936, when it was replaced for the first time.

The mechanism of the clock is not underground but in the plinth of the statue of Allan Ramsay, who gazes benignly from his pedestal above (*see* STATUES). The mechanism is weight-driven and has to be wound every day; it keeps perfect time, being practical as well as beautiful to look at. The hands are 8 and 5 feet long; the circumference of the clock is 36 ft, the width 11 ft 10 in. When filled with plants the weight of the large hand is 80 lbs; that of the small hand is 40 lbs.

At first the cuckoo's song was made by two diapason organ pipes; today it is produced by two tuning valves played through a loudspeaker, and the cuckoo is now made to pop out of a small bird-house above the clock face.

After the success of Edinburgh's Floral Clock the idea caught on all over Britain and ultimately in many parts of the world: India, Australia, New Zealand, the USA, Canada, South America, South Africa and Europe.

Themes of the Floral Clock in the past have included: the Edinburgh Festival, Robert Louis Stevenson, Robert Burns, the Salvation Army and the International Botanical Congress.

The 24000 flowers used in the clock are all dwarf varieties of many colours, and the complex designs take three men around three weeks to plant with Lobelia Waverley Blue, Pyrethrum Golden Moss, Beet, varieties of Echeveria, Sedums, etc.

George V, George VI
Thistle Chapel

The entrance to the Thistle Chapel displays on right and left the list of Knights from 1687 when the Order of the Thistle was revived by James VII. Within the Chapel itself are memorials to:
George V (1868-1936), on the communion table (by John F Matthew, 1943)
George VI (1895-1952), on an inscribed slab in floor (by Esmé Gordon, 1962).

Gordon Highlanders
Castle Esplanade: south side/2nd turret

A bronze plaque surmounted by the stag's head of the regimental crest (in relief) commemorates those who died in the South African War of 1899-1902. The regiment sailed from India in September 1899 to take part in the Boer War. At Elandslaagte the pipers stood in a ring and sounded the charge; Drum-Major Lawrence, the first to reach the Boer guns, put his claymore down the muzzle of one and said 'I capture this gun in the name of the Gordon Highlanders'. Two VCs were awarded as a result of this engagement

At the siege of Ladysmith, which lasted 102 days, the Gordon Highlanders were part of the British garrison. The daily ration of meat was half a pound (horse or mule) and one-and-a-half biscuits per man. They ate berries and used dried tea-leaves as tobacco. At the Relief of Ladysmith the Gordon Pipers played the relief force into the town.

In the Eastern Transvaal in July 1900, during a night of lashing rain, the Highland brigade approached the enemy position and stumbled into barbed wire. They lay all day on the veldt in the burning sun, huge blisters on their knees.

At Houtnek in April Captain Towse, accompanied by seven men, scrambled from rock to rock under fire. They reached a crest and found 150 Boers at only a few yards' range. They were invited to surrender but charged. Captain Towse was shot through the temples, losing the sight of both eyes, but after six hours of fighting, the Gordon Highlanders captured the plateau. Towse was awarded the VC.

At Dornkop, Corporal J F Mackay won the VC for attending to wounded comrades under heavy fire at close range, for dressing wounds himself without shelter and for carrying a wounded man to the cover of a rock. The regiment was authorised to bear on its colours 'South Africa 1899-1902'.

78th Highland Regiment (Indian Mutiny)

Castle Esplanade: north side

A twenty-seven feet high Celtic cross and pedestal in dark Redhall stone, with interlaced tracery and an Indian elephant carved at its base, this memorial was the work of a local sculptor, Mr S Hunter and the wrought-iron railing was constructed by a Farrier-Sergeant at Leith Fort.

The Scotsman of 16 April 1862 records the inauguration: 'The troops formed a hollow square in front of the monument, which was draped by the Royal Standard and the Union Jack. The Royal Artillery, with their field-battery of Armstrong guns, were stationed on the upper part of the Esplanade, the Cameronians on the south, ranged in companies, with officers in front, while the Scots Greys, on horseback, occupied the lower part of the hill. The day was mild and sunny and the portions of the Esplanade not occupied by the soldiers were covered with spectators.

At a signal from Major-General Walker (the Commander of the Forces in Scotland), the monument was instantly uncovered while the troops presented arms and the bands played the National Anthem. The cross at the top was then seen to be surrounded by a wreath formed of laurel leaves and deer's grass (the badge of the Mackenzie Highlanders gathered on the hills of Ross-shire) festooned with blue ribbons. Three hearty hip-hip-hurrahs, led by General Walker, were given by the troops and enthusiastically echoed by the spectators. The band of the Scots Greys then played "Scots Wha Hae" in slow time, and the ceremony was concluded.'

According to the inscription on the cross seven officers, 28 NCOs and 220 privates of the 78th Regiment fell in India.

79th Highlanders

Dean Cemetery: opposite entrance lodge

An obelisk is dedicated to the officers (named on the stone) and 369 non-commissioned officers and men who died in Bulgaria and in the Crimea or fell in action during the Crimean War, 1854-55. The base of the obelisk is carved with the names of two of the battles: 'Alma', 'Sevastopol'.

The International Brigade

East Princes Street Gardens: western embankment

The rough-hewn man-size block of stone erected by Friends of the International Brigade Association has a plaque with the following inscription:

> To honour the Memory of
> Those who went from
> The Lothians and Fife to Serve
> In the War in Spain
> 1936-1939

Not to a fanfare of trumpets,
Nor even the skirl o' the pipes,
Not for the off'r of a shilling
Nor to see their names up in lights.

> Their call was a cry of anguish,
> From the hearts of the people of Spain.
> Some paid with their lives it is true:
> Their sacrifice was not in vain.

Eight men from Edinburgh returned to the city on 11 December 1938 from service with the International Brigade in Spain, only a small section of the 90 Scots who returned.

After arriving in Glasgow by train the Edinburgh and District veterans were given a rousing reception at Waverley Station; a triumphant procession with bands playing and banners waving marched down Leith Street to the Free Gardeners' Hall in Picardy Place where a tumultuous meeting took place, speech after emotional speech, interspersed with singing 'The Internationale' and 'The Red Flag'.

Of the 30 men from Edinburgh and Fife who joined the Brigade, 13 died in action, among them Harry Fry (a commander of the British Battalion) and 18-year-old Johnny Rutherford from Newhaven, who was taken prisoner at Jarama and later executed by firing squad. George Bridges (of the British Section of the International Socialist Labour Party) was killed at Jarama.

Most of the volunteers were between 20 and 30 years of age, with between six months and two years' service in Spain. Among them were: George Drever, son of a Leith shipyard worker, a graduate of Edinburgh University and a metallurgist who later worked for ICI; Councillor Donald Renton, who was taken prisoner in a battle near Madrid, sentenced to death but saved by an exchange of prisoners; Councillor Thomas Murray (a political commissar in Spain) who with his brother George (assigned to anti-tank battery) and his sister Annie (a nurse), fought at Brunete in 1937 and at the Ebro Front a year later, after which the International Brigade was disbanded.

King's Own Scottish Borderers
Castle Esplanade: south side

A plaque commemorates the raising of the King's Own Scottish Borderers on what is now the Castle Esplanade on 19 March 1689 by David Leslie (1660-1728), 3rd Earl of Leven. A thousand men enlisted in the space of two hours.

The Edinburgh Regiment of Foot, as it was first called, was raised to defend the Lowlands against the Jacobite Highlanders fighting in the name of James II (then in France) against William of Orange, who was now on the English throne.

At the Battle of Killiekrankie in 1689 Leven's regiment was one of only two which did not run away before the Highlanders. The Highlanders' leader, John Graham of Claverhouse (1648-89), otherwise known as 'Bonnie Dundee', won the battle but was himself killed.

After the Battle of Killiecrankie the Edinburgh Regiment took the song 'Bonnie Dundee' as its regimental march. On its regimental badge was Edinburgh Castle and the Edinburgh motto 'Nisi Dominus Frustra' (from the Latin version of the 127th Psalm: 'Except the Lord build the house, they labour in vain that build it'). In order to honour its achievement at Killiecrankie, the Magistrates of the City of Edinburgh conferred on Leven's regiment the unique right of recruiting by beat of drum in the city and of marching through the city at any time with drums beating, colours flying and bayonets fixed.

Carolus Linnaeus (1707-78)
Royal Botanic Garden

Carl Linné was a Swedish botanist who established a system for classifying plants and animals. Linnaeus' manuscripts and collections are kept at the Linnean Society, London.

The monument, designed by Robert Adam in 1778, is an oval urn on a square pedestal, with a portrait head in low relief over a Latin inscription. This records that the monument was erected in 1779 by Dr John Hope (1725-60), Regius Keeper for the second Botanic Garden in Haddington Place. Dr Hope was the first to introduce the Linnean system of botanical classification into Scotland.

Nearby is a plaque to Sir Isaac Bayley Balfour, a former Keeper, designed by Sir Robert Lorimer.

Linnaeus Monument

McEwan Lamp

Outside McEwan Hall in Bristo Square

An ornamental marble monument on a granite base; cherubs dance below a magnificent green and gold lamp, the gift of the Rt Hon. William McEwan LLD, MP for Central Edinburgh (1886-1900).

William McEwan, born in Alloa in 1827, was the son of a ship-owner. He worked at first in Glasgow for a commission agent and then as a bookkeeper in a spinning firm in Yorkshire. He came to Edinburgh in 1851 where he started a brewing firm after having had some experience in that line in his uncle's firm, John Jeffrey and Co. Following his great success as a brewer, McEwan became Liberal MP for Central

Edinburgh in 1886 and gave £40000 to buy land. As the subsequent building of a new University hall progressed, McEwan gave orders for more and more elaborate decoration to be carried out, and the final cost to him was some £115000.

On 3 December 1897 the McEwan Hall was opened by the Rt Hon. A J Balfour, Chancellor of the University of Edinburgh. William McEwan died in 1913 aged 86 years.

Colonel Kenneth Douglas Mackenzie CB (1811-73)

Castle Esplanade: north side

Colonel Mackenzie served for 42 years in the 92nd Highlanders and on the staff of the Army in many parts of the world.

As a Captain during the Irish Rebellion in 1848 he was highly commended. In the Crimean War he took part in the battles of Alma, Inkerman and Sebastapol as a Brigade-Major with the Light Division (1854-55). In Bengal he quelled the mutiny of the 5th Bengal European Regiment (1859) and in the following year was Quarter-Master General in China.

He died tragically in 1873 while on manoeuvres on Dartmoor. At the inquest his brother-in-law (who was with him at the time of the accident) gave the following statement (as reported in the *Western Morning News*): 'He had his office at Green Farm during the manoeuvres. At three o'clock we left in a two-wheel trap and I observed that there was an unusual flood in the river. I was driving and we entered the river and had crossed the centre; the horse was evidently getting onto shallow ground up the bank, but stopped. Col. Mackenzie stood to get out but the trap turned over at the moment of his doing so. I was under the trap and on getting to the surface saw him standing up to his middle in the stream holding onto some bushes. On my getting out I ran to him but he let go before I reached him. We both had our uniforms and heavy great coats on: he was carried into the middle of the rapid below but I got him to the bank and said "Thank

God we are all right." He smiled and said "All right."
He walked, leaning on me, about five yards. I saw he
was much exhausted and made him lie down. I then
ran off to get him some brandy. On my return I gave
him some brandy and undid his clothes: he was
evidently dying at the time.'

Col. Mackenzie was interred at Blackleigh with full
military honours.

Martyrs Cross
East end of Grassmarket at the foot of the West Bow

A flat circle of cobblestones with a mosaic of the St
Andrews Cross and the inscription: 'Many Martyrs and
Covenanters died for the Protestant Faith on this
spot.'

The Martyrs Cross was opened in 1937 and paid for
by public subscription to mark the site of the public
gallows where many of the Covenanters were hanged;
James Mitchell was executed in 1676 and James
Renwick in 1688. After public executions ceased in
1784 a large block of sandstone (in which the wooden
gallows was inserted) remained on the site until 1823.
See also: Covenanters Monument (MONUMENTS).

Martyrs of Reform
Old Calton Cemetery

The 90-ft-high obelisk commemorates members of the
Edinburgh Society of Friends of the People, an
electoral reform society founded in 1792 by Thomas
Muir (1765-98). The following year Muir went to Paris,
then in the throes of the French Revolution. There he
met Thomas Paine, American author of *The Rights of
Man*, but on his return to Scotland found he had been
outlawed for sedition and was imprisoned in the
Tolbooth. At his trial he spoke in his own defence for
three hours; he asserted, 'When our ashes shall be
scattered by the winds of heaven, the impartial voice
of future times will rejudge your verdict.' With the
other four reformers Muir was sentenced to 14 years
transportation.

Muir's companions were: William Skirving, a farmer from Fife who had studied Divinity at Edinburgh University; Joseph Gerrald, born in the West Indies, who had practised at the Pennsylvania bar for four years before coming to England in 1788; Maurice Margarot, the only one of the five to return to Britain, who landed at Liverpool in 1810 and died penniless five years later at the age of 70; and the Rev. Thomas Palmer (1747-1802), educated at Eton and Cambridge, then Unitarian minister at Montrose (1783) and Dundee (1785). Having served his sentence, Palmer sailed into the Pacific but died on the island of Guam. His body was later exhumed and taken to Massachusetts.

The obelisk was completed in 1845. When the foundation stone was laid in 1844, 400 members of the Complete Suffrage Association, dressed in black, walked past the High Court, scene of the mis-trial of Muir by the notorious Lord Braxfield. The harshness of the verdict is said to have inspired Robert Burns to compose 'Scots Wha Hae'.

1st Viscount Melville (1742-1811)

St Andrew Square: Parliament Hall

The Melville monument in St Andrew Square is modelled on Trajan's Column in Rome and stands 150-ft high. It was designed by William Burn and erected in 1820-23. A 14-ft statue of the Viscount by Robert Forrest was placed on top of the column in 1822.

Henry Dundas, the first Viscount Melville, was born and bred in Edinburgh. He trained as a lawyer and in his early twenties was made Solicitor-General for Scotland. In 1774 he was elected MP for Midlothian, and in following years William Pitt the Younger chose him for a number of key posts: Treasurer of the Navy, Home Secretary, President of the Board of Control for India, First Lord of the Admiralty and Secretary for War. In time, Dundas gained complete control over the electoral system in Scotland and was known as 'the absolute dictator of Scotland' and 'Harry the Ninth, uncrowned King of Scotland'.

In 1805 his fortunes changed dramatically when he was charged with embezzling funds while Treasurer of the Navy. He was, however, eventually acquitted.

Against the north wall of Parliament Hall stands the statue of Henry Dundas by Sir Francis Chantrey (1818).

Melville Monument

Mercat Cross
High Street: east of St Giles Cathedral

The Mercat Cross marks the place where business was transacted until 1753 when the Royal Exchange (now the City Chambers) was built. From it royal proclamations were made, and on festive occasions the cross had even been known to gush with wine like a fountain.

The Mercat Cross first appears in recorded history in 1365, standing about 50 feet east of the east end of St Giles Cathedral. In 1617 it was taken down to widen the roadway and then re-erected opposite Old Fishmarket Close; the executions of Huntly (1649), Montrose (1650), Wariston (1663) and the Argylls (1661 and 1685) took place there, and there also, after Culloden, the flag of the conquered Prince Charles Edward Stuart was ceremonially burned in public. In 1756 the Cross was removed.

It was re-erected in 1885 by William Gladstone, the Liberal Prime Minister, as a mark of gratitude to the City of Edinburgh; during his first Midlothian campaign of 1880, the citizens had crowded into Princes Street to welcome him and thronged Waverley Market and the Corn Exchange to hear him. The present site of the Mercat Cross (only the capital dates from the 15th century) is some 25 feet short of its position in the 14th century.

Mercat Cross

Heart of Midlothian
High Street: west of St Giles Cathedral

A heart-shaped reminder (made from granite setts) marks the spot in the High Street where once stood the Old Tolbooth Jail with its hated condemned cell. Brass plates outline the plan of the Old Tolbooth and the Luckenbooths built against it. The Heart of Midlothian marks the doorway out of the Old Tolbooth; the custom was for prisoners who had been set free to spit as they passed through the door to liberty.

The hated symbol of the Old Tolbooth also stands under the execution platform. Hugo Arnot, writing in 1778, describes the cells of the Old Tolbooth: 'In the corner of the room we saw, shoved together, a quantity of dust, rags and straw, the refuse of a long succession of criminals. We went to the apartment above, where were two miserable boys, not twelve years of age. But there we had no leisure for observation; for, no sooner was the door opened, than such an incredible stench assailed us, from the stagnant and putrid air as utterly to overpower us.'

Muriel Spark, the Edinburgh-born novelist, has referred to 'the saturnine Heart of Midlothian, never mine!' Sir Walter Scott was present in 1817 to watch the demolition of the Old Tolbooth and the condemned cell: a strong oak chest, iron-plated, nine-feet square, closed by a strong iron door with heavy bolts and locks. The engineer James Nasmyth, who was there with his father (the painter of the well-known portrait of Robert Burns) and Scott, his father's friend, wrote: 'As soon as the clouds of dust had been dispersed, he observed, under the place where the iron box had stood, a number of skeletons of rats, as dry as mummies. He selected one of these, wrapped it in a newspaper, and put it in his pocket, as a recollection of his first day in Edinburgh, and of the total destruction of the "Heart of Midlothian".'

Heart of Midlothian

Heart of Midlothian
Haymarket roundabout

A War Memorial erected by the Heart of Midlothian Football Club to the memory of the players and members who fell in the Great War (1914-18) and in the Second World War (1939-45).

The memorial is in the form of a pylon with two clock faces, the work of H S Gamley (1921-22).

Earl of Moray (d 1332)
Edinburgh Castle: top of Lang Stairs

Thomas Randolph, Earl of Moray, the nephew of Robert I, had at first co-operated with the English after his capture at Methven, but in 1313 he more than compensated for this disloyalty by an exploit glowingly related in the epic poem 'The Brus' (c 1375), by John Barbour (c 1320-95).

Edinburgh Castle had been in the hands of the English for almost 18 years; an English deserter, William Francis, who knew every nook and cranny of the Castle, revealed to Randolph how to climb the Castle walls.

As a boy in the Castle (where his father was part of the garrison), Francis had fallen in love with a Scots girl who lived in the Grassmarket; he had discovered how to get in and out of the Castle at night without being seen. As Barbour puts it:

> 'And giff ye think ye will assay
> To pass up efter me that way,
> Up to the wall I sall you bring,
> Giff God us saves from perceiving
> Of them that watches on the wall.'

With 30 men Randolph and Francis set off up the Castle Rock:

> 'The crag was high and hideous
> And the climbing richt perilous.'

Halfway up the Rock they stopped to regain their breath on a ledge. Suddenly they heard, just above them, the officer of the watch doing his rounds. If they were caught now it was certain death.

The officer walked on, then all at once there came a shout above them: 'Away with you! I can see you well!', and a stone came whistling down past their heads. The Scots said nothing and the English guard laughed at his comrades who had been startled by the joke.

Now the final assault had come. The Scots, using a rope ladder, scaled the outer rampart wall. The English garrison, taken completely by surprise, offered little resistance and in no time the Castle was Scottish again.

National Monument

Calton Hill

In 1822 a proposal was made by a number of public figures, including Sir Walter Scott, Lord Cockburn and Lord Elgin (who had sold the 'Elgin Marbles' from the Parthenon to the British Museum in 1816), to build a monument to the fallen of the Napoleonic Wars. It was to be a copy of the Parthenon, the temple of the goddess Athena on the hill of the Acropolis in Athens.

During his visit to Edinburgh in 1822 George IV laid the six-ton foundation stone of the National Monument, having processed up the Calton Hill with representatives of all the trades, escorted by the Royal Scots Greys. Each of the twelve pillars of Craigleith stone finally erected weighed 10-15 tons and cost £1000.

The monument was intended to form a Hall of Heroes with statues of all the great men and women of Scotland, but the project was undersubscribed and never completed; only half of the £42000 needed was raised from the people of Edinburgh. So one of the most picturesque features of 'The Athens of the North' became popularly known as 'Edinburgh's Folly' and 'Edinburgh's Disgrace'.

National Monument

Nelson Monument
Calton Hill

Designed in 1807 by Robert Burn (in imitation of an upturned telescope), the monument stands 100 ft high with a 30-ft mast; there are 143 steps to the top and the top of the tower is about 500 ft above sea-level.

A plaque at the entrance to the monument records that it was erected by the grateful citizens of Edinburgh 'To the memory of Vice-Admiral Horatio Lord Viscount Nelson, and of the great victory of Trafalgar, too dearly purchased with his blood'. Close by, in one of the garden walks, was a stone inscribed with the following lines by the blind poet John Milton:

'Hither shall all the valiant youth resort,
And from his memory inflame their breasts,
To matchless valour, and adventures high.'

The base of the monument is five-sided and there are six stages surmounted by cross-trees and a time-ball. In winter the time-ball drops simultaneously with the one o'clock gun at the Castle, thus giving a time-signal to shipping in the Firth of Forth. In summer, because the time-ball operates according to Greenwich Mean Time, it drops at 2 pm.

On the plaque can be seen the stern of the captured Spanish ship, the *San Josef*, and not far from the monument stands a 17th-century Portuguese brass cannon, pointing down Princes Street.

The Nelson monument (which on 21 October, Trafalgar Day, is brightly covered with flags reading 'England expects . . .') originally contained many tributes to Nelson; some apartments were set aside for disabled seamen, and the Edinburgh Nelson Club dined in the monument to celebrate the anniversaries of his victories. Lord Cockburn's opinion of the monument was that 'Nothing that sticks up without smoking seems to one ever to look ill in Edinburgh.'

Nelson Monument

Norwegian Brigade
West Princes Street Gardens

An eight-ton, 900-million-year-old granite boulder, put in place by the Norwegian Army in 1978 (the 350th anniversary of the Norwegian Army), is a mark of gratitude for the help given to Norwegians during the Second World War. At that time the Norwegian Brigade was raised in Scotland and many Norwegian officers fought with the 52nd Lowland Battalion of the Royal Scots. At Edinburgh Castle is a copy of the ancient Norwegian sword, 'Snartemo Sverdet', presented by Norway in 1949.

Many Norwegian students have studied at Edinburgh University and Heriot-Watt University; a feature of their presence is the celebration of their national day each year. Traditionally the City of Bergen gives Edinburgh a Christmas tree, which is erected on the Mound and covered in lights.

More personal links have been forged between Norway and Scotland by men such as Christian Frederik Salvesen who came to Leith from Norway in 1851 and helped to establish the flourishing firm of Christian Salvesen plc. Edward, Lord Salvesen (1857-1942) became Solicitor-General for Scotland and was instrumental in founding Edinburgh Zoo, for which he supplied 800 penguins from the firm's whaling-base at Leith in South Georgia on the Falkland Islands.

John Playfair (1748-1819)
Calton Hill: north-east corner of Observatory

John Playfair, the mathematician, was founder and president of the Astronomical Institution. He was the uncle of the architect William Playfair, who designed both the Observatory (1818) and, in memory of his uncle, a monument in the form of a Greek portico on a podium (1825-6).

John Playfair was born in Dundee and educated at the University of St Andrews. An ordained minister, he turned to the academic life and in 1785 became joint Professor of Mathematics at Edinburgh. In 1805 he left that post to become Professor of Natural Philosophy. He is chiefly remembered for his defence of James Hutton's theory of the earth in his *Illustrations of the Huttonian Theory of the Earth* (1802).

Lord Cockburn writes of Professor Playfair that: 'No one who knew John Playfair can ever resist basking in his remembrance. The enlargement of his popularity after he began to verge towards age, was the natural result of the beautiful process by which that most delightful philosopher increased in moral youthfulness as he declined in years.

'Profound, yet cheerful; social, yet always respectable; strong in his feelings but uniformly gentle; a universal favourite, yet never moved from his simplicity; in humble circumstances, but contented and charitable – he realised our ideas of an amiable philosopher.'

Princess Louise's Argyllshire Highlanders

Castle Esplanade: south-west turret

The Argyll and Sutherland Highlanders (as the regiment is now known) originated from a request by George II to the Duke of Argyll in 1794 to raise a regiment for foreign service in the aftermath of the French Revolution, the greater part of the regiment being raised from Edinburgh and Glasgow.

In 1871, at the wedding of HRH Princess Louise to the son of the Duke of Argyll, the regiment formed a guard of honour and was subsequently granted the privilege of bearing on its colour the Argyll Campbell boar's head and the motto 'Ne Obliviscaris' (do not forget).

When the regiment went into garrison at Edinburgh Castle in May 1873 it began, under the direction of Colonel Sprot, an intensive programme of field manoeuvres; route marching was performed every day during the winter and the 91st Highlanders played a very active part in the ceremonial and recreational life of Edinburgh.

The regiment was on duty at the opening of the General Assembly of the Church of Scotland; it provided sentries at the 1874 Royal Scottish Academy exhibition and the officers presented two nights of theatrical entertainment at the Theatre Royal. The *Scotsman* critic observed that 'an amount of histrionic talent was exhibited which was so enjoyable as it is rarely met with at the hands of amateurs'. The result was a donation from the garrison of £50 to the Royal Infirmary and another of £50 to the Royal Hospital for Sick Children. All through the winter of 1873-4 the regimental band and pipers played once a week in the Assembly Music Rooms, a charge of sixpence a head being made for entrance, so that at the end of the winter £42 had been collected which, together with subscriptions from the officers, was used to erect a double fountain and water-trough on the Esplanade close to the cab-stand at the Castle gate. In June 1874 the regiment left Edinburgh.

Royal Scots

West Princes Street Gardens

Designed by Frank Mears and Partners (1950) with low relief carvings by C Pilkington Jackson, the memorial runs from north to south at the east embankment below the Floral Clock.

The oldest regiment in the British Army, the Royal Scots was raised in 1633 by Sir John Hepburn to fight for Louis XIII of France during the Thirty Years War. The regiment later fought at Culloden, helped to defeat Napoleon in Egypt, and saw service at Corunna in Spain, India, the Crimea and South Africa.

Royal Scots Greys

West Princes Street Gardens: on Princes Street

A bronze trooper on horseback, facing the Castle and standing on a rocky plinth, this statue commemorates members of the regiment who died in the Boer War (1899-1902). The sculptor was W Birnie Rhind (1906) and the memorial was unveiled by the Earl of Rosebery in that year.

The regiment had its origins in the troops of Dragoons raised in 1678 under Lieutenant-General Tam Dalyell to suppress the Covenanters. At the time of the Boer War the regiment's Colonel-in-Chief, appointed by Queen Victoria, was the Russian Emperor, Tsar Nicholas II.

Stationed in Edinburgh, the Royal Scots Greys landed in South Africa dressed in new khaki uniform carefully designed for maximum camouflage: even their magnificent grey horses were dyed.

They set off under General French for the relief of Kimberley, losing many horses in the difficult terrain; at the River Modder the Scots Greys also took part in the last-ever full-scale British cavalry charge, which ended in the capture of Kimberley.

At Paardeburg, one of the fiercest encounters with the Boers, at Bloemfontein and at the Relief of Mafeking, the Royal Scots Greys played a significant part. In July 1900 the 'C' Squadron of the Scots Greys was attacked at Ziliket's Neck by the Boers under Paul Botha. After half a day of fighting the squadron had no ammunition left, had lost two officers, one soldier, with a number of wounded. Having let the horses loose, the squadron leader was forced to surrender.

By the time peace was declared in May 1902, the Royal Scots Greys had made almost 400 marches and lost 45000 horses. Seven officers and 67 soldiers had died.

Royal Scots Greys Memorial

Sasine of Nova Scotia

Castle Esplanade: east of drawbridge

The rank of baronet had originally been introduced by King James I and VI as a way of raising money and colonising the provinces of Ulster. Charles I revived the custom in order to persuade settlers to emigrate to Nova Scotia, a territory which had been granted to Sir William Alexander of Menstrie, Earl of Stirling.

The number of baronetcies was to be limited to 150, each baronet paying £3000 for the privilege. To overcome the difficulty of giving rights of possession to a land overseas, the earth and stones of the Castlehill were converted by Royal Mandate into that of Nova Scotia and the new baronets given the rights of castle, pit and gallows in a ceremony supervised by the Lord Lyon and his heralds.

The first baronet was Sir Robert Gordon of Gordonstoun, Morayshire, created baronet on 26 May 1625: between that date and 1649 some 64 baronets took *sasine* (possession) of their Nova Scotia territory.

In January 1943 the Court of the Lord Lyon sent a sack of earth and stone from the Castle and a beam of oak to be incorporated into the Tercentenary Monument at Annapolis.

In October 1953 the Premier of Nova Scotia, the Rt Hon. Angus Macdonald, unveiled a plaque at the Castle Esplanade commemorating the first baronets who received sasine of their 16000-acre estates, and he deposited a handful of earth from Nova Scotia into the dry moat of the Castle.

Scott Monument

East Princes Street Gardens

On 15 August 1840 (the 69th anniversary of the birth of Sir Walter Scott) the foundation stone of the monument was officially laid. The day had been declared a public holiday. The Lord Provost and many dignitaries (including the Earls of Dalhousie and Rothes) were present; a Masonic procession left from the quadrangle of the University and a second body moved from what is now the Royal Scottish Academy, accompanied by dragoons. The end of the ceremony was signalled by the firing of a seven-gun salvo from a battery from the opposite slope of West Princes Street Gardens.

On the evening of 6 March 1844, halfway through the construction of the monument, the architect, George Meikle Kemp, was returning from a visit to the building contractor on the side of the Union Canal in Fountainbridge when he is thought to have slipped in the fog and so fallen into the canal and drowned. His body was discovered a week later. At his funeral, Kemp's coffin was taken by building workers from the Scott Monument to St Cuthbert's Cemetery.

The Scott Monument is just over 200 ft high with foundations lying 52 ft below Princes Street. Reactions to the monument included that of the art historian John Ruskin, who thought it should have been placed on Salisbury Crags: he called it a 'small vulgar Gothic steeple'; Dickens, who often came to Edinburgh, believed that it was a failure: 'It is like the spire of a Gothic church taken off and stuck in the ground!'

Scott Monument

Scottish/American Civil War
Old Calton Cemetery

The 15-ft-high red granite memorial (1893) marks a plot of ground given by the Lord Provost and Town Council to the United States Consul, Wallace Bruce, as a burial-place for five Scottish soldiers killed in the American Civil War (1861-5). The monument was designed by an American sculptor, George E Bissell, and executed by an Edinburgh firm, Stewart, McGlashen & Sons.

The *Scotsman* report of the unveiling of the monument on 21 August 1893 makes it clear that the life-size statue of President Abraham Lincoln which stands on the monument was the first erected in Europe: 'The statue on the monument before them was that of a great statesman who stood up for liberty and the integrity of the empire to which he belonged – (applause) – and he hoped this memorial would remain as an object-lesson to all Scotsmen to exert themselves in like manner in the future. – (applause)': so commented the Chairman of the Monument Committee, Henry R Heath.

The monument has as its subject 'Lincoln Emancipating the Slave' with the bronze figure of a slave resting on battle flags, holding his right hand up to Lincoln in gratitude. Inscriptions are a quotation from Lincoln, 'To Preserve the Jewel of Liberty in the Framework of Freedom', and the motto 'Emancipation, Education, Union, Suffrage'.

Scottish/American 1st World War
West Princes Street Gardens

Unveiled in 1927 and gifted to the people of Scotland by Americans of Scottish blood, the monument is in the form of a 30-ft-long relief of Scots soldiers on the march with a bronze sculpture of a soldier in front. The statue, entitled 'The Call', shows a young soldier sitting with his rifle over his knee and gazing forward in

determination to fight for his country. The work of Dr
Robert Tait McKenzie, a lecturer in anatomy and head
of the department of physical education at Pennsylvania University, the statue is largely modelled on a
young student, Granville Carrel.

The Scottish American Association dates from 1919
when, in the aftermath of the First World War, many
misunderstandings existed between Europe and the
United States. The aim of the Association was to
emphasise the strong historical links between the USA
and Scotland.

Apart from the inestimable contribution that
Scottish emigrants had made to American culture and
industry, Edinburgh had played host to a number of
distinguished Americans, including Benjamin Franklin
(1759 and 1771) and the novelist Henry James (1878),
who wrote: 'Princes Street was absolutely operatic.
The radiant moon hung right above the Castle and the
ancient houses that keep it company on its rocky
pedestal. They looked fantastic and ethereal, like the
battlements of a magician's palace'. General Ulysses
Grant was made a Freeman of Edinburgh in 1877, and
on his visit in 1946 General Eisenhower commented
that 'Cities like Edinburgh, far from being mere
structures of brick and stone, are living symbols of
mankind's fundamental need of faith in co-operative
action'.

Scottish Horse

Castle Esplanade: north-east corner

A red granite Celtic cross stands in memory of officers,
NCOs and men killed in action and who died of
wounds in the South African War 1901-02. The
regimental motto 'Nemo me impune lacessit' ('No one
harms me with impunity' – the motto of Scotland) is
followed by a list of those killed in action (the
Commander of the Second Regiment, ten officers,
eight NCOs, 43 troopers and four Zulu scouts) and of
those killed by accident or disease (two officers, 21
NCOs and 33 troopers).

The Scottish Horse was recruited in South Africa,

mainly from men of Scottish descent, to carry out Lord Kitchener's plan to use large numbers of mounted infantry against the Boers. Four squadrons of 50 special scouts and 50 cyclists, including 250 Australians and 400 men recruited by the Duke of Atholl in Scotland, made up the force which was engaged in clearing the Boers from the mountains and plains.

At the coronation of King Edward VII in 1902 a detachment from the Scottish Horse was present wearing 'the jaunty hat with black cock tail, Tullibardine's desperadoes'. This refers to Captain the Marquess of Tullibardine (later the 8th Duke of Atholl), who, while serving in Natal, had been given the task of raising the Scottish Horse.

Later that year, on 3 September, the Scottish Horse was disbanded at Edinburgh Castle. 100 men stayed in South Africa and joined the Natal Mounted Police, and in the following year the Scottish Horse found new life in a new Home Service Regiment of Imperial Yeomanry.

Scottish National War Memorial

Edinburgh Castle: Hall of Honour

The Scottish National War Memorial commemorates the dead of two World Wars. It is a National Shrine containing memorials to different branches of the Scottish services and, in the Rolls of Honour on the pinnacle of the Castle Rock, a record of those who gave their lives in the Great War.

ENTRANCE PORCH
Reveille

SOUTH WALL
Scots in English, Irish and Welsh Regiments
The Royal Marine Artillery
The Royal Naval School of Music
Royal Marine Light Infantry

WEST CHAPEL
Women's Services
Merchant Marine/Chaplains to the Forces
Cameron Highlanders
Indian Army
Princess Louise's Argyll and Sutherland Highlanders
Nursing Services

WEST WALL
Royal Navy/Royal Flying Corps/RAF

NORTH WALL
Highland Light Infantry (City of Glasgow Regiment)
Cameronians (Scottish Rifles)
Royal Scots Fusiliers, 21st
Scots Guards
Royal Scots (The Royal Regiment)
King's Own Scottish Borderers
Black Watch (Royal Highlanders)
Seaforth Highlanders (Ross-shire Buffs/The Duke of Albany's)

EAST WALL
Navy

EAST CHAPEL
Yeomanry
Royal Artillery
London, Liverpool and South African Scots
Gordon Highlanders
Household Cavalry (Scottish members)
Royal Scots Greys
Royal Engineers
Earl Haig

Scottish Singers
Waterloo Place: Foot of Calton Hill stairs

The bronze plaque commemorates three nineteenth-century singers:

(Scottish Singers)
John Wilson (1800-49)

The son of an Edinburgh stagecoach driver, Wilson worked as a printer for the firm of Ballantyne but on Sundays was a chorister and later precentor in several churches.

In 1830, after study in London, he began an operatic career in the part of Harry Bertram in 'Guy Mannering' in Edinburgh. He moved to London, appearing at Covent Garden till 1835 and then at Drury Lane.

He was most successful, however, in a series of Scottish entertainments ('Jacobite Songs', 'A Night wi' Burns') with which he charmed his audiences all over the world. Queen Victoria, on her visit to the Highlands in 1842, heard him sing at Taymouth Castle and was captivated by his beautiful tenor voice and the expressive style of his singing. America and Canada took him to their hearts and it was in Quebec in 1849 that his career came to an abrupt end when Wilson was one of many victims of an outbreak of cholera in the city.

His burial-place was restored by the other famous Scottish singer, the baritone, David Kennedy. A tall, truncated obelisk in Dean Cemetery, Edinburgh, commemorates Wilson: 'Born Edinburgh, Christmas Day 1800. Died 9th July 1849 at Quebec, where in Mount Hermon Cemetery another obelisk marks his resting-place'.

John Templeton (1802-86)

Templeton came from a family of singers and, though born in Ayrshire, he was brought up in Edinburgh where he sang as a precentor before making his professional debut as an operatic tenor in England in 1828. He appeared at Drury Lane in 1831 and two years later the great Madame Malibran, the Spanish idol of the opera world, chose Templeton to partner her in all of her performances up to the time of her death in 1836.

There are various versions of their relationship: one

says that the two singers tolerated each other; a second that there was a romantic attachment between them. It is said that the brilliant, unhappy Malibran, who never recovered from the effects of a riding accident, at their last performance together gave Templeton her 'richly jewelled betrothal ring'.

With a chest voice of two octaves that had purity, flexibility, sweetness and power, Templeton played over 180 operatic roles, and after a performance of Bellini's 'La Sonnambula' the composer embraced him in admiration. After visiting Paris Templeton turned to a concert career, and toured the USA singing the songs of his native land. He lived to the age of 84 in a suburb of London.

David Kennedy (1825-86)

Kennedy was the son of a Perth precentor and held that post in a number of Edinburgh churches, leading the congregation and singing baritone solos.

He began a concert career in 1860, touring the country and appearing at the Hanover Square Rooms and in the Egyptian Hall, London. Then followed international tours to the USA, Canada, New Zealand, South Africa and India with a repertoire chiefly of the 'Auld Scots Sangs'.

He conducted the Perth Choral Society from its foundation in 1850 and was the father of the Scottish folk-song collector Marjory Kennedy-Fraser, who continued her father's tradition of international concert-tours.

Catherine Sinclair (1800-64)
Corner of North Charlotte Street and St Colme Street

A 60-ft carved Gothic cross in freestone, hexagonal in shape (like a miniature Scott monument), designed by David Bryce and sculpted by John Rhind, this monument commemorates Catherine Sinclair, author and benefactor. She set up a mission-station in the Water of Leith area of Edinburgh and maintained a large industrial school to prepare girls for domestic service; she gave pensions to the elderly, formed a volunteer company of artisans, with its own uniform, drill sergeant and band of music; she was the first to set up a public fountain in the city and the first to introduce cooking depots (one in the Old and one in the New Town) where a dinner of broth, bread and potatoes could be had, and she took a special interest in the welfare of cab-drivers.

Catherine Sinclair, daughter of Sir John Sinclair, the agriculturist and financier, was probably best known for her many children's books, in particular, *Holiday House*, in which she writes: 'In these pages the author has endeavoured to paint that species of noisy, frolicsome, mischievous children, now almost extinct, wishing to preserve a sort of fabulous remembrance of days long past, when young people were like wild horses on the prairies, rather than like well-broken hacks on the road. In this age of wonderful mechanical inventions, the very mind of youth seems in danger of becoming a machine; and while every effort is used to stuff the memory like a cricket ball, with well-known facts and ready-made opinions, no room is left for the vigour of natural feelings, the glow of natural genius, and the ardour of natural enthusiasm'.

Catherine Sinclair died in Kensington, and when her body was on its way to St John's Episcopal Church, Edinburgh, where she is buried, many hundreds of people lined the streets in tribute.

Robert Louis Stevenson Memorial
West Princes Street Gardens

The Memorial Appeal Committee of the Robert Louis Stevenson Club of Edinburgh raised around £60 000 to plant a grove of five birch trees west of the Ross Open Air Theatre. They are enclosed by a stone wall, at its centre a half column with the inscription 'Man of Letters – RLS – 1850-1894'. The memorial is the work of Scots poet and artist Ian Hamilton Finlay. Perhaps the most vivid description of the writer was given by his landlady in San Francisco in 1879: 'He was a strange looking, shabby, shack of a fellow. He wore a little, brown, rough ulster buttoned tight under his chin, and Scotch brogues, the walking kind, laced up high, and his pants stuck in the tops and a dicer hat.'

Stevenson, nicknamed *Tusitala* (Weaver of Tales) in Samoa, had a love/hate relationship with Edinburgh, but the city was never far from his thoughts and its atmosphere inspired much of his work.

Dugald Stewart (1753-1828)
Calton Hill: south-west of the Observatory

Like the Burns Monument, that to Dugald Stewart by William Playfair (1831) is based on the Choragic Monument of Lysicrates in Athens and encloses a stone urn.

Professor of Moral Philosophy at Edinburgh, Stewart was (in Cockburn's words): 'about the middle size, weakly limbed, and with an appearance of feebleness which gave an air of delicacy to his gait and structure. His forehead was large and bald, his eyebrows bushy, his eyes grey and intelligent, and capable of conveying any emotion, from indignation to pity, from serene sense to hearty humour; in which they were powerfully aided by his lips, which, though rather large perhaps, were flexible and expressive. The voice was singularly pleasing; and, as he managed it, a slight burr only made its tones softer. His ear, both for music and for speech, was exquisite; and he was the finest reader I have ever heard. His gesture was simple and elegant, though not free from a tinge of professional formality; and his whole manner that of an academic gentleman.

'To me his lectures were like the opening of the heavens. I felt that I had a soul. His noble views, unfolded in glorious sentences, elevated me into a higher world. They changed my whole nature'.

Dugald Stewart's mausoleum, almost obscured by ivy, is in Canongate churchyard. He died at No. 5 Ainslie Place, Edinburgh.

St Giles Cathedral
High Street

St Giles High Kirk can claim to be the historical focus of the Church of Scotland in stone and mortar – within its walls the Reformers stretched their wings and the passion of sermon and theological debate echoed. Under its arching steeple the glorious dead of Scotland are commemorated, those who achieved in battle or in the effort of artistic creation or in devotion to a common cause of healing or protection.

Eminent Men and Women

WEST WINDOW
Robert Burns (1759-96) lower panels: the world of nature; upper panels: the brotherhood of man (Designed by Icelandic artist Leifur Breidfjord: see also slate square in nave floor: 'poet of humanity')

CHAPEL OF YOUTH
Sir William Smith (1854-1914), founder in 1883 of the Boys Brigade (west wall).
William Chambers (1800-83), Lord Provost, publisher and conservationist.
Dr Sophia Jex-Blake (1840-1912), pioneer of medical education for women.

NORTH CHOIR AISLE
Edward Max Salvesen (d.1915),
Dr Elsie Maud Inglis (1864-1917), pioneering war surgeon.

LOWER AISLE STAIR
Wellesley Bailey (1846-1937), founder of the Leprosy Mission.

PRESTON AISLE
R S Lorimer (1864-1939), architect.
Arthur Penrhyn Stanley (1815-81), dean of Westminster; 'He loved Scotland'.

SOUTH AISLE
Robert Fergusson (1750-74), poet admired by Burns.
Margaret Oliphant (1828-97), novelist.
Dr Thomas Chalmers (1780-1847), founding father of
the Free Church.
Dr John Brown (1810-82), author of *Rab and His
Friends* (1859).

OUTER SOUTH AISLE (west wall)
Robert Louis Stevenson (1850-94), author.

SOUTH AISLE (west wall)
Gen. Sir William Lockart, Indian Army (1841-1900).

CENTRAL PILLAR (south-east)
Gavin Douglas (1474-1522), provost of St Giles
(1501) and poet.

Regimental Memorials

ALBANY AISLE (west wall)
1st World War Chaplains (Ch. of Scot/Unit. Free/Free
Ch.).
Royal Scots (north wall) 17th Rosebery Bat.; 7th Bat.
Royal Scots; 16th (S) Bat.
Royal Engineers, Edin. Field Co: Egypt 1914-18.

NORTH AISLE (north wall)
Royal Scots Fusiliers, 2nd Bat: South African War
1899-1902.
Highland Light Infantry: South African War.
Royal Highlanders, 42nd ('The Black Watch'):
Egyptian Campaign 1882.
Highlanders, 74th: India 1789-1805.
Forth Royal Garrison Artillery 1939-45.
Scottish Sharp Shooters: South Africa 1900-01.
Royal Scots Fusiliers 1914-19.
Seaforth Highlanders, 1st Bat: Internat. Occup. of
Crete/Nile Expedit. 1898.
King's Own Scottish Borderers: India 1875-92.
Duke of Albany's Own Highlanders, 72nd (high on
north wall).

NORTH AISLE (west wall)
Royal Scots, 3rd Bat. Edin. Lt. Inf. Militia: South
African War 1900-02.
Royal Scots Greys, Camel Corps: Abu Klea, Sudan
1885 (gilded Celtic cross).
Queen's Own Cameron Highlanders: South African
War 1900-02.

NORTH CHOIR AISLE
Royal Army Medical Corps: 1st World War (bronze
ministering angel).
Scottish Nurses 1914-19.
HAA Regiment, 94th ('City of Edin.'): 2nd World War.

SOUTH CHOIR AISLE
Chaplains, Ch. of Scot: 2nd World War.

INNER SOUTH AISLE
Royal Scots, 6th Bat: Egypt and France.
Royal Scots: Boer War 1899-1902.
Royal Scots, 5th Bat: 1st World War.
Royal Scots, 9th Bat: 1st World War.
Royal Scots, 4th Bat (Queen's Edin. Rifles): Gully
Ravine, Gallipoli 1915.
Royal Scots, 5th Bat (Queen's Edin. Rifles): Gallipoli
landing 1915.

SOUTH AISLE (west wall)
Sutherland Highlanders, 93rd: Indian Mutiny 1857-
58.
Highland Regiment, 78th: women and children died
on banks of River Indus 1844-45.
Gordon Highlanders, 92nd: Afghanistan and South
Africa.

Sundial
Wall of Ramsay Lodge: Castle Esplanade

Facing the visitor, high above the Witches' Fountain
on Castlehill, is a sundial held by a cherub. It forms
part of the decorative window lintel and bears the date

1892. Around it is a quotation from the Greek dramatist Aeschylus (525-456 BC) taken from his play *The Eumenides* (line 286). *The Eumenides* tells how Orestes (son of King Agamemnon) avenges the murder of his father (by his mother) by in turn killing her. Immediately Orestes is pursued by the horrifically cruel Furies (barbaric witch-like creatures who bring death and punishment). Orestes defends himself by saying that 'Time cleanses all things in ageing them' (the quotation used by Sir Patrick Geddes on the wall of his 'seven-towered castle built for his beloved'). The quotation below in English is from Robert Burns's 'A Man's a Man for A' That':

> Then let us pray that come it may
> (As come it will for a' that),
> That Sense and Worth o'er a' the earth,
> Shall bear the gree, an' a' that.
> For a' that, an' a' that,
> It's coming yet for a' that,
> That Man to Man, the world o'er,
> Shall brothers be for a' that'.

Taken with the inscription on the fountain designed by one of Geddes' designers, John Duncan, the message of the sundial is quite plainly a plea for tolerance and understanding and the putting away of persecution and superstition.

Thomas Telford (1757-1834)

Dean Bridge

In 1957 a plaque was erected by the Institution of Civil Engineers to commemorate the bicentenary of the birth of Telford, the first President of the Institution.

Telford was born in Dumfriesshire in 1757 and worked as a stonemason before coming to Edinburgh in 1779 for two years to work on the New Town. While in Edinburgh he took the opportunity to study its architecture in order to improve his own understanding of civil engineering. To Telford Edinburgh was 'a large city of romantic appearance'. He surveyed the Edinburgh-to-London route on a number of occasions and built the 90-ft span of the Dean Bridge, his greatest stone bridge, at the age of 75, two years before his death.

The Witches' Fountain
Castle Esplanade: west wall

Designed by John Duncan for Sir Patrick Geddes in 1894 and erected in 1912, this stylish bronze drinking-fountain commemorates the 300 witches who were tied at the stake, strangled and then burnt to ashes on the Castlehill between 1492 and 1722.

The purpose of the drinking-fountain is to record the fact that not all witches worked for evil ends; the 'serene head' is Hygiea, goddess of health, and the serpent is the symbol of Aesculapius, god of medicine (still honoured by doctors today). Though the foxglove produces digitalis, it is also a thing of beauty, and the Evil Eye can be counteracted by the Hands of Healing. Through the cleansing fire of the centre panel passed black magicians and also the well-intentioned practitioners of homeopathic medicine. It was King James VI and I (born in Edinburgh Castle) who fuelled popular fear of witches by his book *Daemonologie* (1597). Seven years previously, the King suspected witches had arranged for violent storms to arise while he crossed to Scotland from Denmark.

In the North Berwick witch trial that followed, men and women admitted under torture that 200 witches had sailed on the sea in sieves and danced round a churchyard in the presence of the Devil. One woman confessed to having hung a black toad upside down for three days and collected the venom in an oyster shell.

The suspects had been tortured by being kept awake, by the use of thumb-screws and by having their legs crushed in the 'boot'. Janet Horne, burnt at the stake in 1722, was the last witch in Scotland to be executed, although the persecution of witches persisted in Europe for another 30 years. In all, over four and a half thousand witches were killed in Scotland.

Minor Monuments

Other man-made monuments mark memories or long-forgotten rituals – the *standing stones*, the upright markers of death, trade or battle; the *wells* – healing, nourishing, and the *fountains* – mobile celebrations in spume and spray – each in its own fashion a visible symbol of a moment in history.

Fountains

Festival Square
Holyrood Palace
Lindsay J Gumley (Waverley Bridge)
Ross Fountain (West Princes Street Gardens)
Waverley Market

Stones

Borestone (Church Hill)
Boroughmuir traders stone (Huntly House Museum)
Caiystane (Oxgangs Road)
Camus (Ravenswood Avenue)
Catstane (Glasgow Road)
Rune Stone (West Princes Street Gardens near Castle Esplanade)

Wells

Balm Well (Howdenhall Road)
Bowfoot
Canongate (Queensberry House)
East Crosscauseway
High Street (John Knox's House)
High Street (Parliament Square)
St Bernard's (south bank of Water of Leith)
St George's (south bank of Water of Leith)
St Margaret's (Holyrood Park)
Waterloo (St Leonard's Street)

Statues

William Adam (1689-1748)
National Portrait Gallery: Queen Street

Architect: father of the architects Robert (1728-92), James (1730-94) and John (1721-92).

Adam's main contribution to Edinburgh's architecture was the first Royal Infirmary (1738, demolished 1882) in Infirmary Street; the Drummond Scrolls at Redford House and the Covenanters Monument in Redford Road are parts of the original building. Adam also designed Hopetoun House (his sons finished it). John Adam planned the City Chambers and supervised the construction of Register House.

Albert, Prince Consort (1819-61)
Charlotte Square/Chambers Street/City Chambers

The figure of Prince Albert on horseback was unveiled by Queen Victoria on 17 August 1876. It had been raining the night before but Charlotte Square was at its greenest and the royal dais shone with draperies of red, blue and crimson. The garden had been divided into eight compartments; into these the ticket-holders were shepherded by the High Constables. The band of the 79th Highlanders and a choir entertained the waiting crowd. Ladies' handkerchiefs were waved from many a window at the Hussars and the blue-jackets from HMS Favourite who were marshalling the crowd. At 4 o'clock the Queen arrived and moved in procession to the dais with all the attendant dignitaries. After an opening prayer the band played the chorale 'Gotha', composed by Prince Albert. The Duke of Buccleuch read an address and then the Queen unveiled the statue as the crowd cheered and the band played.

The sculptor, John Steell, who was responsible for a great number of the public statues and busts in the city, was later knighted by the Queen at Holyrood Palace.

The bronze statue of Prince Albert shows him dressed in a Field Marshall's uniform. The base is of Aberdeen granite and the surrounding panels were the work of D V Stevenson ('Science and Learning' and 'Labour') and Clark Stanton ('Army and Navy').

Other scuplutres of Prince Albert can be seen above the entrance to the Royal Scottish Museum in Chambers Street and (a bust) in the main Council Chamber of the City Chambers.

Alexander and Bucephalus
Courtyard of City Chambers

The Emperor Alexander and his horse Bucephalus (literally 'bull-headed'), modelled by Sir John Steell, was the first of Steell's ten Edinburgh statues and the one which brought him to the public eye. The statue represents 'mind over brute force'.

Modelled in 1832, but not cast in bronze until 1883, the work at first was placed in St Andrew Square but was moved in 1917 to its present site in order to make room for a statue of Gladstone.

Ludwig van Beethoven (1770-1827)
Usher Hall: Grand Circle foyer

There are two busts of the great composer, one carved by Louis Meyer (1869-1969) from the USA and presented to the City of Edinburgh in 1970 by Gunther and Ernst Leitz.

Adam Black (1784-1874)
East Princes Street Gardens

The work of John Hutchison (1876-77).

Black was born in Charles Street, Edinburgh and, after attending the High School, was apprenticed to a bookseller. Further experience in the trade followed in London before he returned to open his own premises in Edinburgh on South Bridge.

After initial setbacks, Black prospered and was able to buy the rights to the *Encyclopaedia Britannica* and to a number of Sir Walter Scott's novels; he also involved himself in the publication of the *Edinburgh Review*.

A Liberal, Black was a member of the Town Council, an MP for Edinburgh from 1856-65 and twice Lord Provost.

Robert Blair (1741-1811)
Parliament Hall: east wall

The sculpture is by Sir Francis Chantrey (1815). Blair was born in East Lothian and was a close friend of Henry Dundas (Lord Melville). After graduating from Edinburgh University he became an advocate and built up a considerable practice. In 1789 he was made a depute advocate by Dundas, a post he held till 1806. For some time he was an assessor of the City of Edinburgh. In due course he filled the most important legal positions: Solicitor-General, Dean of the Faculty of Advocates and finally Lord President of the College of Justice (1808). Although possessed of a keen mind he was not blessed with great eloquence.

On 20 May 1811 he died suddenly in his house at No. 56 George Square. Lord Melville, who had come to attend the funeral of his old friend, took ill in the house of his nephew next door and died there on the day of Robert Blair's funeral, their two bodies lying separated only by the house walls.

David Boyle (1772-1853)
Parliament Hall: east wall

A statue by Sir John Steell (1860) commemorates a lawyer distinguished as much for the dignity of his personal appearance as for his legal virtues. Boyle was the fourth son of the third son of the second Earl of Glasgow. In 1807 he was returned as MP for Ayrshire, a position he held till 1811 when he was appointed Lord Justice Clerk. In 1820 he was made a member of the Privy Council of George IV and took part in the latter's coronation; his dress sense on that occasion was remarked upon by Sir Walter Scott. Boyle served as Lord Justice Clerk for almost 30 years until he was appointed President of the Court of Session. He retired in 1852.

Buccleuch, Walter Francis, 5th Duke (1806-84)
Parliament Square

Standing in the robes of the Order of the Garter, Walter Francis Scott, Duke of Buccleuch, Lord Privy Seal (1842-46) and Lord President of the Council (1846), commands the west entrance to St Giles Cathedral, the High Court and the headquarters of Lothian Regional Council. The figure is by J Edgar Boehm (1887-88). More than 10 ft high, it faces west so as to get most light. It is carved of stone from the Binny Quarry as it was thought this would weather better than granite and blend well with the bronze panels. The whole design was the work of Dr Rowand Anderson.

On the hexagonal base of the statue are six bucks rampant holding the arms of families allied by marriage with the Buccleuchs. Six relief panels by Clark Stanton show incidents in the Buccleuch family history:

1. Sir Walter Scott (1389-1402), 4th Lord of Rankeillor and Murthocton, falls in battle at Homildon Hill.
2. Lady Buccleuch (Elizabeth Kerr of Cessford), widow of Sir Walter (1492-1504), burned by the English in Catalack Tower on Yarrow, 1548.
3. Attempted rescue by Buccleuch of James V from the power of the Earl of Angus 1526.
4. The burning of Branxholme Tower by the English, 1532.
5/6. Two scenes from the ballad of Kinmont Willie, 1596.

Six symbolical figures of the virtues of the Duke (Fortitude, Liberality, Temperance, Prudence, Charity and Truth) are by W Birnie Rhind, while the panels of incidents in the 5th Duke's life are by Stuart Burnett:

1. Receiving Queen Victoria at Dalkeith in 1842.
2. Planning Granton Harbour (building began in 1835).
3. Anniversary dinner given by his tenants in Edinburgh in 1877.
4. His installation as Chancellor of Glasgow University.
5. His service as Colonel of Militia.
6. The Duke's coat of arms.

Robert Burns (1759-96)
Bernard Street, Leith/National Portrait Gallery

Burns is commemorated by two life-size statues: one, in marble by John Flaxman (1755-1826), originally stood in the chamber at the base of the Burns Monument at Regent Road (see *MONUMENTS*) and is now in the Main Hall of the Scottish National Portrait Gallery, Queen Street; the other, in bronze by D W Stevenson (1898), stands in Bernard Street, Leith, facing west up Constitution Street to Edinburgh. The poet is depicted holding a plaid on his shoulder.

Stevenson's statue was the gift of the Leith Burns Club; around the red sandstone base are four bronze plaques illustrating Burns quotations:

1. 'The priest-like father reads the sacred page'
   'From scenes like these old Scotia's grandeur springs,
   That makes her loved at home, revered abroad'
2. 'When Vulcan gies his bellows breath
   An' plowmen gather wi' their graith'
3. 'I there wi' something did forgather,
   That put me in an eerie swither'
4. 'In order, on the clean hearth-stane
   The luggies three are ranged'

The first panel is a domestic scene; the second a blacksmith's shop; in the third the poet meets Death with his scythe; the fourth shows the game of 'dookin' (ducking) for apples at Hallowe'en.

Burns' best-known appreciation of Edinburgh is in his poem:

'Edina! Scotia's darling seat!
All hail thy palaces and towers,
Where once beneath a monarch's feet
Sat Legislation's sovereign powers.'

Thomas Carlyle (1795-1881)
National Portrait Gallery

Sir J E Boehm's dignified seated figure of Carlyle is a reminder that he studied at Edinburgh University as a future candidate for the church, but turned instead to school mathematics teaching. He then returned to Edinburgh to study law (with no success), and took up writing. It was in Edinburgh that he met his future wife, Jane Welsh, and after their marriage they settled in the city for ten years until 1825. In 1865 Carlyle became Rector of Edinburgh University.

Andrew Carnegie (1835-1919)
Edinburgh Central Library: upper landing

The work of Charles McBride (1891), the bust of Carnegie is a memorial to his generosity to the city. Carnegie was born the son of a Dunfermline linen weaver. He emigrated to Pittsburgh, USA, in 1848 and carved out a living for himself on the railways, later working in heavy iron and steel production, eventually becoming one of the richest men in the world.

He donated £50000 to pay for the construction of a public library system in Edinburgh. The Carnegie Library in George IV Bridge is a monument to his understanding of the importance of reading for pleasure and for information.

Thomas Chalmers (1780-1847)
George Street: Castle Street intersection

The sculptor, Sir John Steell, made a bust in 1847; the present bronze statue on a red granite base dates from 1878.

Son of a general merchant, ship-owner and dyer, Chalmers was born in Anstruther and studied mathematics at St Andrews and natural philosophy at Edinburgh University.

He had, meantime, begun to study for the ministry, and in 1799 he gave his first public sermon in Wigan. Four years later he was appointed a lecturer in mathematics at St Andrews. Having been ordained a minister he started his own extramural classes in mathematics and chemistry in St Andrews.

In 1823 Chalmers became Professor of Moral Philosophy in St Andrews and, in 1828, Professor of Divinity at Edinburgh. In 1834 he was awarded a doctorate in Civil Law by the University of Oxford.

Dr Chalmers' greatest achievement was still to come; the contradictory strands of his academic career came together in 1843 and over a point of church law. A ruling of the Court of Session made it clear that a lay patron had the right to choose a minister for a parish regardless of the wishes of the congregation. Dr Chalmers disagreed, believing that the Church must be separate from the State. Chalmers marched out of the General Assembly with 470 other ministers (out of a total of some 1200) in what became known as 'The Disruption', creating the Free Church of Scotland.

William Chambers (1800-83)
Centre of Chambers Street

The statue of Chambers was executed by John Rhind (1888-91). On three sides of the red sandstone plinth are graceful female figures by Hippolyte Blanc representing Literature, Liberality and Perseverance.

Originally from Peebles, William Chambers (with his brother Robert) moved to Edinburgh where he became apprenticed to a bookseller who lent books and sold lottery tickets.

In due course William and Robert (1802-71) set up as booksellers and then moved into printing, producing in 1821 their first joint venture, a periodical called *Kaleidoscope*, written by Robert and printed by William. It lasted only a year.

A vast quantity of publications followed from both brothers: *Chambers Edinburgh Journal*, the *Biographical Dictionary of Eminent Scotsmen* (1833-35), *Songs of Scotland prior to Burns* (1862) and Robert Chambers' invaluable collection of oral memories, *Traditions of Edinburgh* (1824).

Following his election as Lord Provost (1865) William Chambers was responsible for many civic improvements, initiating slum clearance, building new streets and widening the High Street closes; Chambers Street is named after him. He personally paid for much of the renovation in St Giles Cathedral and was responsible for many of the imaginative features of the restoration. His funeral service was the first service to be held in the restored Cathedral.

Charles II (1630-85)
Parliament Square

Between the entrance to the High Court and the south wall of St Giles Cathedral is the six-ton lead statue of King Charles II, mounted on horseback and dressed as a Roman general wearing a victor's laurel wreath. Robert Louis Stevenson commented sardonically that 'a bandy-legged and garlanded Charles Second made of lead, bestrides a tun-bellied charger'. The statue was first erected on that site, at a cost of £2580, in 1685, before Charles's death. It has constantly required repair. In 1834, for example, the internal supports gave way, and it was taken away shortly before the great fire of November 1924 which destroyed the south side of the High Street and much of Parliament Square. The statue spent the next nine years stored in the Calton Jail.

It has not been without controversy or mystery. In 1767 the City Fathers had it painted white, much to the amusement of the population and of James Boswell in particular, who penned a humorous poem on the subject.

There are at least three versions of the statue's origin: the authorised one is that it was cast in Holland and shipped to Edinburgh from Rotterdam. Another claims that it was originally that of the Duke of Parma, later recycled; the last tradition is that it was first erected during the Commonwealth (1649-53) as Oliver Cromwell on horseback. At the Restoration the statue was taken down to be sold as scrap but a local builder bought it, stored it away and, having decapitated it and replaced the head, sold it back to the city. What cannot be disputed is the fact that it is the oldest equestrian lead statue of its kind in Britain.

Charles II

Prince Charles Edward Stuart (1720-88)
City Chambers

'Bonnie Prince Charlie', the Young Pretender, captured the City of Edinburgh with Highland sleight of hand, captured the hearts of the ladies and set a romantic fashion for tartan.

The Prince rode into the Palace of Holyrood on 17 September 1745 to a rapturous welcome from 20000 citizens. 'He was in the prime of youth, tall and handsome, of a fair complexion; he had a light-coloured periwig, with his own hair combed over the front. He wore the Highland dress, a tartan short coat without the plaid, crimson velvet breeches and military boots; a blue bonnet was on his head and on his breast the Star of the Order of St Andrew.' After a remarkably well-mannered occupation of the city, the Prince left the capital of Scotland on 1 November never to return.

Behind the Provost's chair in the Council Chambers stands the statue of Prince Charlie; the Young Pretender is shown as a Roman Emperor. The statue is believed to have been made in France, to have been shipped from Dunkirk and on its arrival in Leith, dropped into the harbour, where it was left under water for some time. It was then taken to the surface and put in a large wooden box; it came to light in 1810 in St Giles Cathedral.

The *Scots Magazine* continues the story: 'some gentlemen connected with the town caused the mysterious box to be opened, and, to their surprise and gratification, they found it contained a beautiful statue of His Majesty, about the size of life, cast in bronze.'

A statuette of the Prince is also one of the central figures on the first gallery of the Scott Monument, facing north.

Fryderyk Chopin (1810-49)
Usher Hall: Grand Circle foyer

The bust of Chopin honours a composer from a nation which has a special place in the heart of Scotland, particularly Edinburgh, for several reasons: Edinburgh has a sizeable Polish community of ex-service personnel; several generations of Polish doctors have been trained at the Polish Medical School in Edinburgh; and Scotland and Poland share a tradition of trading links.

It was a Polish GP, Dr Adam Lyschinski, in whose home at No. 10 Warriston Crescent Chopin lived during his visit to Edinburgh in 1848. The brilliant pianist and composer was suffering from ill health and the after-effects of his estrangement from the French woman novelist George Sand. Chopin felt the biting Edinburgh wind and had difficulty in warming his hands before playing the piano; he composed a song in the city, 'The Spring', perhaps a gesture of hope during a period of profound despair. He gave one concert only, in the Hopetoun Rooms at the west end of Queen Street (now Erskine House and at one time Mary Erskine School) on 4 October 1848. 'The infinite delicacy and finish of his playing', wrote the *Scotsman*, 'combined with great occasional energy never overdone, is very striking when we contemplate the man – a slender and delicate-looking person, with a marked profile, indicating much intellectual energy'.

Henry Cockburn (1779-1854)
Parliament Hall: north-east corner

The fine statue of Cockburn is by William Brodie (1863).

Cockburn in his writings is the conscience of Edinburgh, a shrewd observer of people and a concerned citizen. Trained as a lawyer, he pursued a wide variety of causes, helping to found the Commercial Bank on the one hand, and the Edinburgh Academy, as a rival to his own High School (which he detested) on the other. He took part in the Burke and Hare case of 1828, defending Burke's wife. From 1830 to 1834 he was Solicitor-General for Scotland and assisted in the drafting of the First Scottish Reform Bill.

He contributed regularly to the *Edinburgh Review* (edited by his friend Francis Jeffrey), in which he is described as 'rather below the middle height, firm, wiry and muscular, inured to active exercise of all kinds, a good swimmer, an accomplished skater, an intense lover of the fresh breezes of heaven. He was the model of a high-bred Scotch gentleman. He spoke with a Doric breadth of accent. Cockburn was one of the most popular men north of the Tweed.'

The Cockburn Association, active today in preserving and developing what is best in the heritage of the city, is called after him and among his descendants were the journalist Claud Cockburn and the novelist Evelyn Waugh.

George Drummond (c 1687-1766)
Edinburgh Royal Infirmary: main entrance hall

Drummond was born in Perthshire; his skill with calculations led to his appointment in 1707 as Account General of Excise at the young age of 20. By 1715 he was Commissioner of Customs.

In the ranks of the Edinburgh Town Council his rise was equally meteoric: City Treasurer (1717), Dean of Guild (1722), Lord Provost (1725). Drummond also involved himself in the General Assembly of the Church of Scotland and, because of the control which the Town Council had over education, he took a leading part in the appointment of many of the outstanding professors at the University of Edinburgh.

Drummond played a key role in establishing the Edinburgh Royal Infirmary (near Drummond Street) and was present at the laying of the foundation stone in 1738. He had fought at the Battle of Sherrifmuir in 1715 on the side of the Hanoverians, and during the 1745 Rebellion he commanded the First (or College) Company in defence of the town, but his men proved to be too timid to go beyond the West Port. However, his experience of military conflict no doubt made him more than ever aware of the need for proper medical care, such as the New Infirmary offered.

His outstanding contribution to Edinburgh (he held the office of Lord Provost for six terms) was in his efforts to create a New Town to the north of the overcrowded Old Town. Before his death Drummond saw the draining of the Nor' Loch (now Princes Street Gardens), the construction of a modern Royal Exchange (now the City Chambers), the erection of a concert hall (St Cecilia's Hall in the Cowgate), and in 1763 he laid the foundation stone of the North Bridge. Ten years after his death the plan for Edinburgh's New Town was finally completed.

Edward VII (1841-1910)
Holyrood Palace/Victoria Park, Newhaven Road

The north and south sides of Holyrood Palace Yard are formed by a Scottish National Memorial to Edward VII designed by G W Browne (1920-22). In a recess of the north-west corner is a bronze statue of the King by H S Gamley with the inscription: 'in memory of Edward, King and Emperor of India 1901-10, his Scottish subjects have erected this memorial in grateful and loyal remembrance.'

The 9-ft-high statue was unveiled by King George V on Tuesday 10 October 1922 in the course of a two-hour visit to the city.

At the east side of Victoria Park, facing Newhaven Road, is a bronze statue of Edward VII, sculpted by John S Rhind (1913). The king is dressed as a member of the Order of the Thistle.

In the hall of the old Royal High School stood a bust of King Edward VII as a young man when he was coached by the Rector of the Royal High School. His father, Princes Albert, wrote: 'Dr Lyon Playfair is giving him lectures in chemistry . . . The Rector of the Royal High School gives him lectures in Roman history; Italian, German, and French are advanced at the same time, and three times a week the Prince exercises with the 16th Hussars, who are stationed in the city.'

Henry Erskine (1746-1817)
Parliament Hall

A bust by Peter Turnerelli (1774-1839) of the Lord Advocate whom Cockburn described as: 'A tall and rather slender figure, a face sparkling with vivacity, a clear sweet voice, and a general suffusion of elegance. In his profession he was the very foremost. No rival approached him in the variety, extent or brilliance of his general practice. Even the old judges, in spite of their abhorrence of his party, smiled upon him; and the eyes of such juries as we then had, in the management of which he was so agreeably despotic, brightened as he entered. Nothing was so sour as not to be sweetened by the glance, the voice, the gaiety, the beauty, of Henry Erskine.'

Kathleen Ferrier (1912-53)
Usher Hall: Grand Circle foyer

A portrait of the outstanding contralto who appeared in the Edinburgh International Festival's 1947 performance of Mahler's 'Song of the Earth' and J S Bach's 'B Minor Mass' in the following year in the Usher Hall. In 1951 she gave a Lieder recital there and in 1952 she sang in Elgar's 'Dream of Gerontius' and again in Mahler's 'Song of the Earth'.

Duncan Forbes (c 1644-1704)
Parliament Hall: East wall

The first and the most magnificent marble statue in Edinburgh of a commoner, Roubiliac's noble and delicately chiselled statue shows Forbes laying down a judgment rather like the Greek Father of the Gods, Zeus.

Forbes was born near Inverness on the family estate and educated in that city. His father, who owned the estate of Culloden, was MP for Nairnshire. Duncan Forbes, a hard drinker and speculator in his youth, studied law at Edinburgh and Leiden and in 1709 became Sheriff of Midlothian. Although a Highlander, he was a supporter of the Hanoverian monarchy. In 1722 he was elected MP for the Inverness burghs and in 1735 he succeeded to the family estate at Culloden.

Two years later Forbes was Lord President of the Court of Session and immediately set about making the Scottish legal system more efficient. At the time of the 1715 Rebellion he worked hard to prevent it ever taking place and, when it did, he quickly took steps to stop more clans joining the Old Pretender's side.

After the defeat of the Jacobites, he saw to it that the prisoners were tried, not in England, but in Scotland; he opposed the intervention of the House of Lords in cases of forfeiture of estates where the Scottish Court of Session had already ruled. This seemed to be against the Treaty of Union which promised that the Court of Session would be independent and apart from the English legal system. He also objected to the Disarming Act of 1716 which made it unlawful for Highlanders to carry weapons of any kind.

Forbes was known as 'King Duncan', so powerful and respected did he become, and at the time of the Porteous Riots, when the English Parliament was determined to strip the Lord Provost of office, abolish the Town Guard and demolish the Netherbow Port, Forbes stood firm for the love of his country.

Duncan Forbes

George II (1683-1760)
Royal Infirmary: north front entrance

The figure of George II as a victorious Roman general wearing a laurel wreath, pointing with his general's baton, bears the inscription:

'George II Brit. Rex, by whom a Royal Charter was granted to the Infirmary of Edinburgh. August 25th 1736'.

George II was the last British monarch to appear in battle (at Dettingen in 1743); he was also a patron of musicians.

In 1775 the statue was placed in a niche on the second floor of the old Royal Infirmary (in Infirmary Street) above the centre doorway. That niche is now at Redford Road built into the 'Drummond Scrolls' containing parts of the facade of William Adam's Royal Infirmary of 1738 (demolished 1884). On each side of the original alcove was a tablet reading: 'I was naked, and ye clothed me' and 'I was sick, and ye visited me'.

George III (1738-1820)
Register House: in west alcove of the Rotunda

The sculpture of the monarch in marble, by Anne Seymour Damer (1795), is tucked into an obscure corner; the figure wears a large brass crown and holds a long brass sceptre.

George III is said to have visited Edinburgh before he became King, lodging at Boyd's White Horse Inn off St Mary's Street (also patronised in 1773 by Dr Samuel Johnson). From the 1780s George III suffered bouts of madness and by 1811 he was permanently insane.

Mrs Damer, the sculptress (1749-1828), was a relative of Horace Walpole and a friend of Nelson and Napoleon; her mother was the daughter of the 4th Duke of Argyll.

George IV (1762-1830)
Intersection of Hanover and George Streets

The visit of George IV to Edinburgh in 1822 was a landmark in the relations between Scotland and the monarchy. The events were stage-managed by Sir Walter Scott; the King descended on Edinburgh like a sun-god and threw himself into the role with enthusiasm.

It was the first visit to Scotland by a ruling British monarch since Charles II in 1650. George IV filled the vacuum left in Scotland by the departure of the monarchy to London in 1603 with symbolism and pageantry designed to appeal to the Scots, who longed for the return of former greatness.

The King arrived at Leith to a tumultuous welcome; there were receptions at Holyrood Palace at which the King paraded dressed in tartan, and a magnificent procession took place to Edinburgh Castle in which George IV carried the recently rediscovered 'Honours of Scotland', the Crown, the Sceptre and the Sword of State.

The Royal Visit was commemorated in a variety of ways, including the naming of a new thoroughfare from the High Street as 'King George IV Bridge', and the erection of an imposing statue by Sir Francis Chantrey (1831) in George Street, facing Princes Street and the Castle.

William Ewart Gladstone (1809-98)
Coates Crescent Gardens

Originally intended for its present site in 1902, the placing of the monument was opposed by the owners and it was set on the west side of St Andrew Square from 1917-55. When it became an increasing hazard to traffic, the monument was moved to its present location.

Designed by J P MacGillivray, the bronze monument shows Gladstone dressed in Chancellor's robes. Below, to east and west, are allegorical female figures representing History and Eloquence. Around the base of the statue are four biblical female figures: Fortitude (holding a cloth bearing the image of the face of Christ), Vitality (with a lamp), Faith (with the Bible), Measure (with a balance). At the front (south), two boys hold up a large laurel wreath and an inscription in Greek.

Gladstone's Edinburgh connections were strong: his father's family was from Leith and it is said that he was connected with the Thomas Gledstanes who bought Gladstone's Land in the Lawnmarket in 1617.

During the winter of 1880, in his first Midlothian

campaign, he drew enormous crowds to see him pass through Princes Street and to hear him speak in the Waverley Market and in the Grassmarket Corn Exchange.

He opened the Scottish Liberal Club in Edinburgh that year (the table on which he wrote his speeches is still there); in his second term of office as Prime Minister his bust was placed there. He also paid for the re-erection of Edinburgh's Mercat Cross in the High Street (*see* MONUMENTS).

Lord Rosebery unveiled the memorial and reminded his audience of the Midlothian campaign and of Gladstone's service as Liberal Prime Minister (1868-74/1880-85/1892-94).

The 'Golden Boy'
Edinburgh University Old College dome

On top of Rowand Anderson's Old College dome (1887) stands the gilded sculpture of an athlete carrying the torch of learning. The work of John Hutchison, it is said to have been modelled on the Edinburgh athlete, Anthony Hall.

Greyfriars Bobby
Junction of George IV Bridge and Candlemaker Row

A bronze statue of the loyal terrier by William Brodie (1872).

Bobby was a trained police dog and helped his master, PC John Gray, protect the livestock at the weekly Wednesday markets held in the Grassmarket. When John Gray died in 1858 his faithful dog spent his days on his master's grave in Greyfriars Cemetery and sheltered at night under a nearby table gravestone.

John Traill, proprietor of the Refreshment Room just around the corner from Greyfriars, fed Bobby during his long 14 years of watching at his master's grave.

In 1867 Bobby was licensed by the Lord Provost and his statue by William Brodie was later erected by Baroness Burdett-Coutts opposite the entrance to the cemetery, with a drinking-fountain beneath.

An account of Greyfriars Bobby, along with his dinner dish, collar and the drinking-cup from the fountain, can all be seen in Huntly House Museum in the Canongate.

Greyfriars Bobby

Thomas Guthrie (1803-73)
West Princes Street Gardens

A figure in Portland stone by F W Pomeroy (1910).

Born in Brechin, Guthrie studied at Edinburgh University, also taking instruction in surgery and anatomy from Dr Robert Knox (who was to find notoriety through his part in the Burke and Hare 'body-snatchers' case) before going to Paris to further his medical education. What he saw in Paris opened his eyes to the depths of human degradation.

He had been licensed to preach in 1852 and, after returning to Edinburgh, he worked first in a bank before becoming a minister in Forfar. Like Dr Thomas Chalmers, Guthrie opposed the patronage system in the appointment of ministers. When the Disruption took place he was one of the leaders of the Free Church, and it was from his church, Free St John's (in the West Bow), that he began his crusade for a system of Ragged Schools which would provide shelter, training and education for the many hundreds of children who roamed the streets of Edinburgh, learning the lessons of crime and brutality.

Hugh Miller supported his first *Plea for Ragged Schools* (1847), which was followed by two more in 1849 and 1860. By 1847 three Ragged Schools were active but it was not till 1866 that a new Industrial School Act was finally passed by Parliament.

Dr Guthrie was a preacher of distinction and a Christian who fought to put his ideas into practice and to provide security and stability to many hundreds of children who would otherwise have had little chance of survival.

He was Moderator of the Free Church in 1872, a manager of the Edinburgh Royal Infirmary, and worked on behalf of the Blind Asylum and the Night Refuge. The effectiveness of his work is not diminished by the fact that the single homeless are still an all-too-common feature of Edinburgh life.

Earl Haig (1861-1928)
Castle Esplanade: north side

A gilded bronze statue of Douglas, 1st Earl Haig, advancing over a rough rock base, faces to the south. It is the work of G E Wade (1922-23).

Born at No. 24 Charlotte Square, Haig was educated at Oxford and the military academy of Sandhurst (1883). He served in India with the 7th Hussars and promotion came quickly; he was with the Egyptian cavalry in the Omdurman campaign in 1869 and was later a Brigade-Major during the Boer War.

By 1903 he was Inspector-General of Cavalry in India, then a Major-General. Haig became Director of Military Training at the War Office in 1906 and three years later was back in India as Chief of the General Staff. As Commander-in-Chief in France during the 1st World War he became the target for heavy criticism levelled at strategies which needlessly caused huge loss of life among the British infantry. After the war Earl Haig worked tirelessly for the British Legion and the United Services Fund in the after-care of injured veterans; symbolic of this work was his institution of the distribution of poppies for Remembrance Sunday.

The statue was the gift of Sir Dhunjibhoy Bomanji, who took a particular interest in Daniel Stewart's College which he visited several times to see a young Parsee boy. Sir Dhunjibhoy gave £200 to the school and £1000 towards a new Edinburgh maternity hospital. He also contributed to the Earl Haig Fund for ex-servicemen and often spoke of his admiration for Earl Haig. In September 1923 he was present at the formal unveiling of the statue. As a boy Sir Dhunjiboy was weak and sickly; his doctor sent him to the strongman Sandow. At the end of a year he could lift a man with both arms simultaneously. He gave Sandow a cheque for £10000 and bought him a house.

George Heriot (1563-1623)
George Heriot's School/Heriot-Watt University

A life-size statue of George Heriot ('Jinglin' Geordie') stands on the north entrance tower rear wall. The memorial, by Robert Mylne, bears a Latin inscription meaning: 'This statue shows my body, this building shows my soul'. In the cemetery of the Greyfriars Kirk he and his brother erected a richly carved monument to their father, also a prosperous goldsmith, against the east wall.

George Heriot followed his well-to-do father into the goldsmith's trade, working from a shop near the north-east corner, and later to the west side, of St Giles. In 1597 he was appointed goldsmith to Anne of Denmark, Queen of Scotland, and in 1601 Jeweller to the King. He also acted as a cashier and banker, lending vast sums to King James VI and his Queen.

When the court moved to London in 1603, Heriot went also and continued to satisfy the royal passion for diamond rings, ambergris, civet and musk. Heriot pawned jewels for the Queen, who could only find the money to repay the 'Scottish Croesus' by obtaining a parliamentary grant of £20000.

Heriot had purchased a great deal of property and after his death his executors continued to buy more in

Edinburgh. Dying childless, Heriot left his fortune to charitable purposes, notably the construction of a 'Hospital and Seminary of orphans for education, nursing and upbringing of youth, being poor orphans and fatherless children of decayed burgesses and freemen of the burgh, destitute and left without money'.

Building began in 1628, but it was not till 1659 that the Hospital began to function as its founder intended. In 1885 the Hospital became George Heriot's School; in many parts of the city other subsidiary schools built by the Heriot's Trust can still be seen, converted now to other uses.

There is a bust of George Heriot above the main entrance to the Heriot-Watt building in Chambers Street.

David Octavius Hill (1802-70)
Scottish National Portrait Gallery ambulatory/Dean Cemetery

A bust of the photographic pioneer by Patric Park stands in the Scottish National Portrait Gallery's Ambulatory on the first floor above the Main Hall. An equally fine bust (now green with age) by his wife Amelia Robertson Paton (1820-1924) marks their joint grave in the Dean Cemetery.

John Hope (1765-1823)
St Andrew Square: Royal Bank of Scotland

The 4th Earl of Hopetoun, in a bronze by Thomas Campbell (planned in 1824 and erected in 1834), stands, dressed as a Roman general in front of his grazing horse.

A long-serving career army officer, Hope took over as Commander-in-Chief at Corunna during the Peninsular campaign when Sir John Moore was mortally wounded. In 1812 he was next in command to the Duke of Wellington and earned the latter's admiration.

Hope was MP for Linlithgowshire in 1790, Governor of the Royal Bank of Scotland, and was admired (in the words of the inscription) for his 'unshaken patriotism', his 'spirit of honour' and his 'skill in the art of war'.

Henry Irving (1836-1905) and Ellen Terry (1847-1928)
King's Theatre foyer

The busts of Sir Henry Irving and Dame Ellen Terry were originally set up in the Royal Lyceum Theatre, Grindlay Street, for the opening of that theatre on 10 September 1883. Executed by D W Stevenson, they show the two 'stars' of their profession who played the leading roles in the theatre's first production, Shakespeare's *Much Ado about Nothing*.

After some spontaneous choral singing by the audience the iron safety curtain went up to show a fine maroon curtain; the orchestra then took their places and to a selection of Scottish airs the curtain was drawn aside to reveal a classical group of figures painted in grey enclosed by a drapery of blue and yellow. After some speeches came the play, during which Irving (his real name was John Henry Brodribb) and Ellen Terry charmed the audience.

Irving had first come to Edinburgh in 1857 when only 19 years old and spent two years at the Theatre Royal. In 1859 the Theatre Royal, Shakespeare Square (where the GPO now is), gave its last performance. Irving played the part of Soapy in *Masks and Faces* and Charles in the farce *His Last Legs* and was praised as a painstaking performer but given to mannerisms. At the Royal Lyceum he played some of his most famous roles: Hamlet, and Mathias the Polish Jew in *The Bells* who, under the influence of the hypnotist in the court scene, relived his crime.

He stayed in the Edinburgh Hotel opposite the Waverley Bridge and also lodged in Robert Burns's old room in St James Square. Irving was often to be seen in a rough, loose-fitting, pepper-and-salt tweed suit, studying his parts as he walked up Arthur's Seat or on the Calton Hill.

James V (1513-42) at Cramond Bridge
Braehead Mains, Queensferry Road

The Craigleith stone sculpture, by Robert Forrest, of
the King attacked by a robber at Cramond Brig, was
completed about 1836. The theme of the memorial is
taken from the well-known play *Cramond Brig, or The
Gudeman of Ballengeich*, often performed in Edinburgh from 1826. James in disguise was attacked by
thieves at Cramond Brig and was rescued by Jock
Howison who had been threshing grain close by.
Without knowing his identity, Howison took James
into his home, washed his wounds and was rewarded
with an invitation to Holyrood Palace; there he was
granted the lands of Braehead in perpetuity, and from
that time the family of Howison Crawfurd kept the
tradition of presenting the reigning monarch with a
towel and basin.

Francis Jeffrey (1773-1850)
Parliament Hall: east wall

Another of Sir John Steell's fine portraits (1855).
    Like his friend Lord Cockburn, Francis Jeffrey was
educated at the High School of Edinburgh: at the age
of 13 he happened to see Robert Burns in the street
and was deeply impressed by the dark glint of the
poet's piercing eye.
    While a student at Oxford he carried a drunken
James Boswell (Dr Johnson's biographer) up to his
rooms and, having helped a fellow Scot in distress,
found that Oxford was full of 'pedants, coxcombs and
strangers'. Jeffrey came back north with an accent
changed from the broadness of Scots to the sharp and
narrow Oxford accent.
    Although he practised as a lawyer at the Scottish
Bar, Jeffrey's energy was most devoted to literature. In
1802, with a group of friends at his flat in Buccleuch
Place, he founded the *Edinburgh Review*, which was
to play such an influential role in the criticism of
Romantic poets like Wordsworth and Byron. In 1830
he was made Lord Advocate.

King's Own Scottish Borderers
North Bridge: east side

Four life-size freestone sculptures commemorate the officers, NCOs and men of the regiment who gave their lives between 1878 and 1902.

A central figure of an officer holding binoculars is accompanied by three others, two holding rifles, one wearing a balaclava. The sculptor was William Birnie Rhind (1853-1930), who completed the work in 1906.

Afghanistan (1878-80): the friendship of the Ameer of Afghanistan with the Russians led to the Second Afghanistan War. The KOSB were part of a column which saw active service in the Khyber Pass.

Egypt (1888-89): after the murder of General Gordon the Second Battalion helped to secure the defeat of the Dervish army.

Chin Lushai (1889-90): the First Battalion spent seven hard months in Burma on a punitive expedition against the Chins and Lushais.

Chitral (1895): action was seen on the North-West Frontier to preserve the great caravan routes and the fertile plains of India from tribal raids. One of the many engagements by the KOSB (with the Gordons) was a hill assault: 'It was a fine and stirring sight to see the splendid dash with which the two Scottish regiments took the hill. From valley to crest at this point the height varies from one thousand to one thousand five hundred feet and the slope looks for the most part almost perpendicular. It was this very steepness which partly accounted for the comparatively small loss suffered from the enemy's fire and the shower of huge boulders which were hurled upon the assailants.' The regiment also took part in the Relief of Chitral.

Tirah (1897-98): 23 actions on the Peshawar and Kohut borders, mostly on top of icy hills with little food and no kit.

South Africa (1900-02): in May 1901 a small column was passing near the Magaliesberg hills; a veldt fire was raging when suddenly, out from the smoke, there appeared 500 Boer horsemen under the support of heavy fire. Two British guns were captured and quickly turned on the column by the Boers. However, companies of the KOSB rescued the column, captured the guns again and drove the Boers back. The Boers vanished into the smoke of the burning veldt.

John Knox (c1512-72)
St Giles Cathedral/New College

Against the north wall of St Giles is to be found the dark bronze figure of Knox by J Pittendrigh MacGillivray (1904-05). It was formerly located at the south wall of the church in Parliament Square and near Knox's grave (parking-space No. 44 in Parliament Square). The statue shows the great reformer, Bible in hand.

A more dramatic bronze of Knox is to be seen in the quadrangle of New College and the Assembly Hall on the Mound. Here is the Old Testament prophet with flowing beard and arm uplifted in warning, an inspired orator.

Knox, buried in St Giles churchyard some years after it was closed, was the figurehead of the Reformation in Scotland. A Catholic priest and Papal notary, he was an expert in Canon Law: his skill in public speaking was sharpened by his legal training.

Cast in the mould of the Old Testament prophets, Knox was born near Haddington in East Lothian. The executions of the Scottish reformers, such as Patrick Hamilton in 1528 and George Wishart in 1546, hardened his resolve that the Church in Scotland needed reformation. In this task he looked to the English Reformed Church for support.

After the assassination of Cardinal Bethune (Beaton) at St Andrews in 1546, Knox arrived to help the Reformed community there as a Protestant minister, teaching and preaching. When St Andrews Castle was captured by the French Knox was made a galley-slave for two years, until the intervention of King Edward VI resulted in his release.

In England he was a minister at Newcastle, Berwick and London before being appointed a Royal Chaplain; he advised Archbishop Cranmer on his drawing up of the Articles of Religion and on the Second Prayer book.

During the reign of the Catholic Queen Mary John Knox was in Frankfurt and Geneva, absorbing the Reformed theology of Calvin. In 1559 he returned to Scotland, becoming minister of St Giles. In the *Book of Discipline* (1560 and 1578) he set out a far-reaching plan for a church without bishops, a programme of universal comprehensive education and a system of poor relief. Against Mary Queen of Scots Knox was a powerful and vocal opponent, exercising a hypnotic gift for public denunciation and prophetic criticism. In England Knox wrote his *History of the Reformation in Scotland* (1587). He came back to Scotland in 1572 and preached in St Giles for the last time.

David Livingstone (1813-73)
East Princes Street Gardens

At a public meeting in the City Chambers on 14 April 1874 a number of people spoke in support of having a statue erected to the missionary and explorer after a design by Mrs D O Hill.

Bishop Cotterill, the Chairman, said that he had been Bishop for 14 years in that part of the Cape Colony which had been the basis of Livingstone's operations. Dr Livingstone was probably the great hero of their generation, a typical Scotsman in his perseverance, and it would be a disgrace to the metropolis of Scotland if it did not erect a memorial to so heroic a man.

The last they had heard of Livingstone was that almost a year previously he had been lying in a hut, fed only with pain, blind at the last and sad, and there he died. His body was now approaching their shores and there was to be a great and honourable funeral.

Professor Blackie pointed out that there was no town in Europe more fitted for the exhibition of sculpture than Edinburgh. In Edinburgh they had thousands of situations sufficiently clear of the crowded population to be marked out for public statues. If Edinburgh were filled with statues this would stir the minds of strangers in a way no guidebook could. Livingstone was a man made of iron and Mrs D O Hill had been fortunate enough to secure a likeness of Dr Livingstone when he had last been in this country. Dr Livingstone was a Freeman of the City of Edinburgh.

Mary Queen of Scots (1542-87)
National Portrait Gallery

A replica of Mary's effigy from her tomb in Westminster Abbey dominates the centre of the Main Hall. The original was made in 1606-12 by Cornelius and William Cure and the tomb built by the order of Mary's son, King James.

Her hands joined in prayer, Mary lies in white on a white and gold tomb, with the red royal lion at her feet holding the symbols of monarchy.

The Scottish National Portrait Gallery also has a bronze bust of the Queen attributed to Jacquio Ponzio (c1561).

2nd Viscount Melville (1771-1851)
Centre of Melville Crescent

Robert Dundas, the son of Henry Dundas, 1st Viscount Melville, is commemorated in a bronze statue on a stone plinth by Sir John Steell (1857).

Melville, like his father, was a lawyer and a staunch Scottish Tory. Lord Cockburn recalls that 'The rise of Robert Dundas, Lord Melville's son, was an important event for his party; for, without his father's force, or power of debate, or commanding station, he had fully as much good sense, excellent business habits, great moderation, and as much candour as, I suppose, a party leader can practise.'

Dundas became MP for a number of English constituencies and then, in 1800, MP for Midlothian. He was President of the Board of Trade, Secretary for Ireland and First Lord of the Admiralty (as his father had been before him). He also held the position of 'Manager for Scotland', which meant that he exercised great control over the Scottish electoral system.

William Pitt (1759-1806)
Intersection of George Street and Frederick Street

The bronze statue of William Pitt the Younger by Sir Francis Chantrey which stands on its stone plinth, facing Edinburgh Castle, was financed by the 600 members of the Edinburgh Pitt Club in 1833.

Pitt was Prime Minister on two occasions (1783-1801 and 1804-6) and the youngest Prime Minister in British history. The huge public debt he inherited in 1782 when he became Chancellor of the Exchequer was reduced by a policy based on the ideas of Adam Smith (who is buried in Edinburgh's Canongate Cemetery). Pitt was largely responsible for two coalitions against France and solved the crisis created by the Irish rebellion in 1798 by uniting Britain and Ireland. Under Pitt the Tories once again entered government.

Henry Raeburn (1756-1823)
National Portrait Gallery ambulatory

A bust by Thomas Campbell.

Raeburn was the son of a yarn-boiler, orphaned at the age of six and educated at Heriot's Hospital. He was apprenticed at 15 to a jeweller and goldsmith but his talent for drawing was first recognised by a seal-engraver, David Deuchar, who happened to visit the workshop. Deuchar gave Raeburn painting lessons and also an introduction to David Martin, then the leading portrait painter in Scotland. In time Raeburn established himself in succession to Martin as the most sought-after portraitist in the country. He trained in London and Rome and worked in Edinburgh from 1787 at his studio in George Street and then at 32 York Place. He produced over 600 portraits and was a man of wide-ranging interests: mechanics, archaeology, golf, gardening and archery.

When George IV made his triumphal visit to Scotland in 1822 Raeburn was knighted at Hopetoun House.

Allan Ramsay (1686-1758)
West Princes Street Gardens

A Carrara marble figure by Sir John Steell (1865), with portrait medallion of Ramsay's family on the plinth, presiding over the Floral Clock.

Born in Leadhills, Lanarkshire, Allan Ramsay was apprenticed to an Edinburgh wig-maker but was so successful in writing songs and poems that he took up bookselling at No. 155 High Street, selling his own *Scots Songs* (1719), *The Tea Table Miscellany* (1724-27) and his best work, *The Gentle Shepherd* (1725), a play.

In 1726 he moved to new premises on the first floor of the Luckenbooths, and his shop was nicknamed 'The Hub of the Universe'. He started the first circulating library in Scotland (1724) in Leadhills, and in 1736 opened a theatre in Carrubbers Close which was shut by the magistrates the following year.

Ramsay lived in his 'goose-pie' octagonal house at Ramsay Gardens (directly above the site of his statue) and owned much of the land below his house. He was a Jacobite and when Prince Charles Edward Stuart captured Edinburgh in 1745, Ramsay retired to the country while the Jacobite army used his house to shoot at the Castle.

Robert I (1274-1329)
Beside Edinburgh Castle entrance

Robert the Bruce (with William Wallace) was the architect of Scottish independence from English rule. Himself from a Norman family, Bruce had a claim to the Scottish throne, and though at first he had fought for the English King Edward I against the Scottish King John Balliol, Bruce, seeing Wallace's powerful stand against the English, took up the fight in 1298.

Appointed Guardian of Scotland, Bruce was one of the leaders of the patriotic movement in Scotland. However, when he saw that John Balliol might be restored as King, Bruce again sided with the lesser of two evils, Edward I of England.

In 1305, shortly after the barbarous execution in England of the heroic William Wallace, Bruce made up his mind to confront Edward I. He had himself publicly enthroned at Scone in the following year. Despite early reverses Bruce fought back doggedly with all the cunning of a resistance fighter. At the Battle of Bannockburn (23-24 June 1314) Bruce, blocking the way to Stirling Castle, shattered the overwhelmingly larger English force under Edward I, using the Scottish *schiltrom* (a variation of the Roman technique of squares bristling with spears like a porcupine). It was not till 1328, however, that Edward III at last signed the Treaty of Edinburgh with Bruce, recognising Scotland's independence.

On 28 May 1929 the statue of King Robert I by Thomas J Clapperton was unveiled by HRH the Duke of York (later King George VI) to commemorate the 600th anniversary of the granting of the earliest surviving royal charter by Robert I in 1329. Signed at Cardross, the charter confirmed in the people of Edinburgh their rights in the burgh, over the Port of Leith and over the many mills in what is now the Dean Village.

Sir Walter Scott (1771-1832)
Scott Monument: East Princes Street Gardens/ National Portrait Gallery/Parliament Hall

Sir John Steell's Carrara marble statue (1846) of the author shows him (double life-size) simply dressed, holding a book, with his deerhound Maida at his feet. At the inauguration Steell announced that 'In being commissioned to execute the statue which has this day been placed in that beautiful, fairy-like tower in the centre of the metropolis of our native land – deeply, very deeply did I feel the importance of that commission, for it not only implied the honour of having a part in the execution of a nation's gratitude to one of the most gifted of her sons, but it implied also the sacred honour of handing down to posterity the lineaments of one whose memory will be cherished by ages yet to come and nations yet unknown.'

Among the statuettes of historical figures on the monument itself are:

James VI (upper tier) by D W Stevenson
George Heriot (lower tier) by Peter Slater
Robert Bruce (upper tier) by George A Lawson
Richard the Lionheart (upper tier) by Mrs Hill
Queen Mary (lower tier) by D W Stevenson

Statuettes added in 1881:

Queen Elizabeth by W Walker
Graham of Claverhouse by W B Rhind
Oliver Cromwell by W Brodie
Duke of Montrose by D W Stevenson
Charles I by D W Stevenson
John Knox by John Rhind
George Buchanan by John Rhind
Rob Roy by John Rhind

Two other major statues of Scott can be found in Edinburgh: a bust by Sir Francis Chantrey in the Main Hall of the National Portrait Gallery, and the freestone statue by John Greenshields (modelled 1832, carved 1835) in Parliament Hall, which is said to be the best likeness of any statue of Scott.

Scottish National Portrait Gallery
Queen Street

Established in 1889, the Portrait Gallery was funded by J R Findlay, the owner of the *The Scotsman*, as a Scottish Pantheon. Among the many sculptures of historical figures on the exterior of the building are:

Admiral Adam Duncan (1731-1804)
David Hume (1711-76)
Adam Smith (1723-90)
James Hutton (1726-97)
Sir Henry Raeburn (1756-1823)
John Napier (1550-1617)
John Barbour (c1320-95)

William Dunbar (c1460-1514)
Gavin Douglas (1474-1522)
Sir David Lindsay (c1486-1555)
John Knox (c1512-72)
George Buchanan (1506-82)
Cardinal Bethune (Beaton) (c1494-1546)
John Campbell, 2nd Duke of Argyll (1678-1743)
King Alexander III (1241-86)
King James I (1394-1437)
King James V (1512-42)
James Stewart, Earl of Moray (1531-70)
King James VI and I (1566-1625)

The sculptors were: W Birnie Rhind, John Hutchison, W G Stevenson, C McBride and Pittendrigh MacGillivray.

Sir James Young Simpson (1811-70)
West Princes Street Gardens

The bronze figure of Sir James Young Simpson, the discoverer of the anaesthetic properties of chloroform, sits and surveys the passing world. The work of William Brodie, the statue was erected in 1876.

Born in Bathgate, Simpson began his studies at Edinburgh University when he was 14. By the time he was 28 he had become Professor of Midwifery, and on 4 November 1847, at his home at No. 52 Queen Street, he and his assistants were experimenting with a number of substances and finally turned their attention to a small bottle of chloroform: 'Immediately an unwonted hilarity seized the party; they became bright-eyed, very happy and very loquacious. The conversation was of unusual intelligence and quite charmed the listeners. But suddenly there was a talk of sounds being heard like those of a cotton-mill, louder and louder; a moment more, then all was quiet, and then – crash.'

Simpson also founded the modern practice of gynaecology and attended Queen Victoria at the birth of Prince Leopold. He was made a baronet in 1866.

St Michael
Edinburgh Castle: Scottish National War Memorial

The painted wooden figure of the Archangel hangs suspended over the casket with its Rolls of Honour. The statue is the work of Alice Meredith Williams.

Standing Group
West Princes Street Gardens

'The Genius of Architecture crowning the Theory and Practice of Art', by William Brodie for his son-in-law, James Gowans, for his house 'Rockville' in Napier Road. The statue was presented to the city in 1871.

Demolished in 1965 amid great controversy, 'Rockville' was a bizarre mansion built with decorated stonework which gave it an oriental appearance.

Andrew Usher (1826-98)
Usher Hall: Grand Circle foyer

A bust by H S Gamley, who was also responsible for the medallion portraits of poets and composers over the entrance doors.

Andrew Usher, a member of a well-known brewing family, financed the building of the Usher Hall with a gift of £100000.

Queen Victoria (1819-1901)
RSA/Leith Walk/City Chambers

The statue of the Queen (1844) by John Steell was described at the time of its unveiling as 'colossal' as it was nearly four times life-size. The *Edinburgh Evening Post* commented: 'We can see an English lady; and accordingly the artist has conveyed that sweet and placid smile which marks the feminine character in its elevated aspect. The entire statue is thus embued with all the majesty which belongs to the office of the Sovereign, rendered interesting and attractive by the gentle and natural expression which belongs to the woman. It is, in fact, impossible to look upon this production without admiration and love – a sentiment which has been freely and warmly expressed by all who have seen it.' Others noted that the new statue of the Queen on the roof of what is now the Royal Scottish Academy (at the foot of the Mound) dwarfed the sphinxes at its side and made them look like kittens.

At the foot of Leith Walk is the figure of the Queen by John S Rhind (1907). To it were added in 1913 the panels showing the arrival in 1842 of the Queen and Prince Consort at Leith and the departure of the volunteers for the South African War (both also by J S Rhind). Some 750 men had volunteered, of whom 298 were chosen to go to South Africa with the 5th V B Royal Scots; with one exception they all returned home.

Marble busts of Queen Victoria and Prince Albert stand in the main Council Chambers at the City Chambers and there are small portrait heads of both set above the entrance to the Chambers Street Museum.

A further statue of the Queen was once placed in Holyrood Palace Yard, but the Queen took an instant dislike to it and replaced it with the present fountain. As for the unfortunate statue, it found its way eventually to the Queen's Theatre where it was destroyed some time later in a fire.

William Wallace (c 1270-1305)
Beside Edinburgh Castle entrance

Wallace, of all fighters for national independence in the late Middle Ages, is unquestionably the most heroic. Hating oppression and the occupation of his native land by a foreign power, he became the focus of a popular Scottish uprising against the English.

For eight years (between 1297 and his execution in 1305) the 'General of the Army of Scotland' fought against English rule. In 1297 he defeated the Earl of Surrey at Stirling Bridge and was appointed Guardian of Scotland. He invaded Northumberland but was later defeated by Edward I at Falkirk. At this point Wallace receded into the background; he went to France to try to enlist the continuing support of the French King for the Scottish cause and looked to the Pope for help against the English. On his return to Scotland, France and the Pope deserted him. Edward I took control once more and in 1305 William was betrayed to the English, tried quickly in London and then executed by hanging, disembowelling and beheading.

The place of William Wallace in the soul of Scotland is best expressed in Burns's song, 'Robert Bruce's March to Bannockburn':

'Scots, wha hae wi' Wallace bled,
Scots, wham Bruce has aften led,
Welcome to your gory bed,
Or to Victorie!'

In May 1929 the statue of William Wallace by Alexander Carrick was unveiled by HRH the Duke of York (later King George VI).

James Watt (1736-1819)

Heriot-Watt Building: Chambers Street. (There are plans to move this statue to the entrance complex of the Heriot-Watt University at Riccarton.)

Holding a book and a set of dividers on his knee, Watt sits beside the entrance, in a bronze by Peter Slater (1854) copied from the seated figure by Sir Francis Chantrey. Above the main door are busts of Leonard Horner and George Heriot, and the keystones of the old Phrenological Museum (incorporated in the building) are to be seen above the bay window to the left of the entrance. They are portraits of men famous in phrenology.

Although Watt was born in Greenock and spent much of his life either in Glasgow or later in England, he had strong ties with Edinburgh. When Joseph Black moved to Edinburgh to become Professor of Chemistry he still continued to have his apparatus made and supplied by Watt, and this meant that Watt often came to Edinburgh on business between 1769 and Black's death in 1799.

Watt visited the Friday Club, meeting Lord Cockburn and Francis Jeffrey, and was also a member of the Cape Club; in this way he grew to know many of the influential men in Edinburgh, such as Lord Brougham (who was later to compose an epitaph on Watt for his monument in Westminster Abbey), Leonard Horner and Sir Walter Scott (who met him in 1814).

In 1783 Watt was elected a Fellow of the Royal Society of Edinburgh, and in 1852 the Edinburgh School of Arts (founded by Horner and the first mechanics' institute in Britain) was renamed the Watt Institution by the City of Edinburgh as a memorial to Scotland's most famous engineer and inventor.

Duke of Wellington (1769-1852)
Princes Street: east end in front of Register House.

The first of the metal castings for the statue by Sir John Steel took place at the end of May 1849 at the foundry built specially for the Wellington statue in Grove Street.

In mid June the enormous statue of Wellington on horseback (weighing twelve tons) was towed by thirty men and eight horses early in the morning to its site. The bright bronze glittered in the sun as the public ceremony took place on 18 June, the anniversary of the Battle of Waterloo. A public holiday had been declared; the city was packed with onlookers.

The 79th Highlanders were in single file along the North Bridge, their plumes easily visible above the heads of the crowd; the 7th Hussars were placed along Princes Street, the North and South Bridges and Waterloo Place. Every roof was covered with people perched on platforms.

A large Masonic procession passed from the University to Register House, led by the Duke of Buccleuch who made a speech on the life of the Duke of Wellington. Then the statue was unveiled to the applause of the crowds and the accompaniment of the military bands who played 'See the Conquering Hero

Comes' and to the stunning noise of the guns at the Castle answered by a battery on the crest of Salisbury Crags.

James Grant the novelist wrote that many 'met on that day who had not seen each other since Waterloo, and when the band struck up "The Garb of Old Gaul" and "The British Grenadiers" many a withered face brightened and many an eye grew moist. Staffs and crutches were brandished and cheering broke forth again and again.'

Duke of Wellington

John Wilson (1785-1854)

East Princes Street Gardens

The bronze statue, which stands on a granite plinth, is by Sir John Steell.

Born in Paisley, Wilson was educated at Glasgow University and Magdalen College, Oxford. He was a fine athlete and travelled extensively in the British Isles before settling near Lake Windermere. He married and, as financial problems arose, he moved to his mother's house in Edinburgh in 1815 and became an advocate shortly after, although he had little success in that field.

Wilson was a talented journalist; after writing about Lord Byron in the *Edinburgh Magazine* in 1817 he began to contribute articles to Blackwood's *Maga*, a Tory publication. *Maga* specialised in satire, attacking poets such as Keats and Coleridge. Better known as 'Christopher North', Wilson wrote *Noctes Ambrosianae*, a series of dramatic dialogues supposed to have taken place at Ambrose's tavern in West Register Street.

In 1820 Wilson managed (largely because of his Tory politics) to have himself elected Professor of Moral Philosophy at Edinburgh University. This was a subject he knew next to nothing about, and he had to rely on letters from an old friend for his lecture-notes, with comical results.

Wilson describes a fishing trip: 'Let us get out of Edinburgh. Here, since November, we have been harbouring among houses, till we have almost hardened into stone and lime. Our system has got smokified; and, a queer fish at all times, you might take us now for a dried haddock!' (1865).

B R Haydon recalls that 'Wilson looked like a fine Sandwich Islander who had been educated in the Highlands. His light hair, deep sea-blue eyes, tall athletic figure, and hearty handgrasp, his eagerness in debate, his violent passions, great genius, and irregular habits, rendered him a formidable partisan, a furious enemy, and an ardent friend.'

Woman and Child
Festival Square, Lothian Road

The bronze statue by Ann Davidson of Aberdeen was unveiled on 22 July 1986 at the height of the boycott of the Commonwealth Games over Britain's policy towards South Africa.

The statue commemorates South Africa's freedom fighters and was unveiled by Mrs Suganya Chetty, a member of the African National Congress born in South Africa but living in exile in Edinburgh for the previous ten years.

Duke of York and Albany (1763-1827)
Castle Esplanade: north side

Frederick, Duke of York and Albany, stands in the robes of a Knight of the Garter, holding a Field Marshall's baton as Commander of the British Army, in a bronze statue by John Greenshields (c1792-1838). Greenshields, son of a small farmer on a Lanarkshire estate belonging to the brother of John Gibson Lockhart (1794-1854), the son-in-law and biographer of Sir Walter Scott, was a stonemason to trade but aspired to be a sculptor. His statue of Scott in Parliament Hall is said to be a very fine likeness. His bronze of the Duke of York was first made for an exhibition in Edinburgh and erected on the Esplanade in 1836, standing, as the nursery-rhyme about the 'Grand Old Duke of York' says, at 'the top of the hill'.

As Commander-in-Chief of the British Army against the Revolutionary French in Flanders during the campaign of 1793 he began well, capturing Valenciennes and being acclaimed King of France; but a series of tactical blunders led to his recall in December 1794 and evacuation from Dunkirk. In 1799 he was again Commander of the British Army in Holland when they were joined by 10000 Russians who advanced too eagerly, causing an unexpected engagement on unfamiliar ground. The result was a humiliating negotiation and withdrawal. Such events produced popular derision, as in the familiar nursery-rhyme, and even Wellington (then a young soldier) confessed many years later that 'I learnt what one ought not to do, and that is always something!'

Off the field of battle, the Duke of York was an able and successful administrator, building up the British Army into a force which would enable Wellington to defeat Napoleon.

FINDING YOUR WAY ABOUT

Monuments

Old Town

Monument	Location
Albany, 72nd Duke's Own Highlanders	Castle Esplanade
Black Watch	The Mound
George V	Thistle Chapel
George VI	Thistle Chapel
Gordon Highlanders	Castle Esplanade
78th Highlanders	Castle Esplanade
King's Own Scottish Borderers	Castle Esplanade
Mackenzie, Col Kenneth	Castle Esplanade
Martyrs Cross	Grassmarket
Mercat Cross	High Street
Heart of Midlothian	High Street
Moray, Earl of	Edinburgh Castle
Princess Louise's Highlanders	Castle Esplanade
Sasine of Nova Scotia	Castle Esplanade
Scottish Horse	Castle Esplanade
Scottish National War Memorial	Edinburgh Castle
St Giles Cathedral	High Street
Sundial	Castle Esplanade
Witches' Fountain	Castle Esplanade

Southside

Brassfounders of Leith	Nicolson Square
McEwan Lamp	Bristo Square

New Town

Monument	Location
Burns, Robert	Regent Road
Floral Clock	West Princes Street Gardens
Highlanders, 79th	Dean Cemetery
International Brigade	East Princes Street Gardens
Linnaeus, Carolus	Royal Botanic Garden
Martyrs of Reform	Old Calton Cemetery
Melville Monument	St Andrew Square
Midlothian, Heart of (War Memorial)	Haymarket Roundabout
National Monument	Calton Hill
Nelson Monument	Calton Hill
Norwegian Brigade	West Princes Street Gardens
Playfair, John	Calton Hill
Royal Scots	West Princes Street Gardens
Royal Scots Greys	West Princes Street Gardens
Scott Monument	East Princes Street Gardens
Scottish/American Civil War	Old Calton Cemetery
Scottish/American 1st World War	West Princes Street Gardens
Scottish Singers	Calton Hill Stairs
Sinclair, Catherine	North Charlotte Street/St Colme Street
Stevenson, Robert Louis	West Princes Street Gardens
Stewart, Dugald	Calton Hill
Telford, Thomas	Dean Bridge

Outer Edinburgh

Covenanters Monument	Redford Road

Statues

Old Town

Statue	Location
Albert, Prince	City Chambers
Alexander and Bucephalus	City Chambers
Blair, Robert	Parliament Hall
Boyle, David	Parliament Hall
Buccleuch, 5th Duke	Parliament Square
Charles II	Parliament Square
Charles, Prince	City Chambers
Cockburn, Henry	Parliament Hall

Statue	Location
Edward VII	Holyrood Place
Erskine, Henry	Parliament Hall
Forbes, Duncan	Parliament Hall
Haig, Earl	Castle Esplanade
Jeffrey, Francis	Parliament Hall
Knox, John	St Giles Cathedral/New College
Robert I	Edinburgh Castle entrance
Scott, Sir Walter	Parliament Hall
St Michael	Edinburgh Castle entrance
Victoria, Queen	City Chambers
Wallace, William	Edinburgh Castle entrance
York, Duke of and Albany	Castle Esplanade

Southside

Albert, Prince	Chambers Street
Beethoven, Ludwig van	Usher Hall
Carnegie, Andrew	Edinburgh Central Library
Chambers, William	Chambers Street
Chopin, Fryderyk	Usher Hall
Drummond, George	Edinburgh Royal Infirmary
Ferrier, Kathleen	Usher Hall
George II	Royal Infirmary
Golden Boy	Edinburgh University Old College dome
Greyfriars Bobby	Junction of George IV Bridge and Candlemaker Row
Heriot, George	George Heriot's School/Heriot-Watt University
Irving, Sir Henry	King's Theatre foyer
King's Own Scottish Borderers	North Bridge
Terry, Dame Ellen	King's Theatre foyer
Usher, Andrew	Usher Hall
Victoria, Queen	Chambers Street Museum
Watt, James	Heriot Watt Building, Chambers Street
Woman and Child	Festival Square, Lothian Road

New Town

Adam, William	National Portrait Gallery
Albert, Prince	Charlotte Square

Statue	Location
Black, Adam	East Princes Street Gardens
Burns, Robert	National Portrait Gallery
Carlyle, Thomas	National Portrait Gallery
Chalmers, Dr Thomas	George Street
George III	Register House
George IV	Hanover/George Streets intersection
Gladstone, William	Coates Crescent Gardens
Guthrie, Dr Thomas	West Princes Street Gardens
Hill, David Octavius	Scottish National Portrait Gallery Ambulatory/ Dean Cemetery
Hope, John	St Andrew Square
Livingstone, David	East Princes Street Gardens
Mary Queen of Scots	National Portrait Gallery
Melville, 2nd Viscount	Centre of Melville Crescent
Pitt, William	George/Frederick Streets intersection
Raeburn, Henry	National Portrait Gallery ambulatory
Ramsay, Allan	West Princes Street Gardens
Scott, Sir Walter	Scott Monument, East Princes Street Gardens/ National Portrait Gallery
Simpson, Sir James Young	West Princes Street Gardens
Standing Group	West Princes Street Gardens
Victoria, Queen	Royal Scottish Academy
Wellington, Duke of	East End of Princes Street
Wilson, John	East Princes Street Gardens

Outer Edinburgh

Statue	Location
Burns, Robert	Bernard Street
Edward VII	Victoria Park
James V	Braehead Mains, Queensferry Road
Victoria, Queen	Leith Walk